Praise for *Bloody Mary's Guide to Hauntings, Horrors, and Dancing with the Dead*

"A journey to the corridor of spiritual experience! Bloody Mary's supernatural side of New Orleans is both fully documented with history and rich with the magic act of invocation through storytelling. Recommended not only for the adept, but also for students of metaphysics, paranormal enthusiasts, practicing spiritualists, and those who need to see how to extend motherly love beyond the human realm."

—Yeye Luisah Teish, author of *Jambalaya: The Natural Woman's Book of Personal Charms and Practical Rituals*

"New Orleans is a place with a colorful history shrouded in dark mystery. Ghosts and voodoo are a part of daily life, and who better to tell you the stories than Bloody Mary, the Voodoo Queen of New Orleans. Mary doesn't just tell the stories of the Big Easy—she lives them. She bridges the world of the living with the realm of the dead, and takes you on this thrilling, lifelong journey of hers in this book."

—Brad Klinge, lead investigator on *Ghost Lab*, Discovery Channel, producer/star of 9 Diamond Productions' *Strange Curiosity*, and co-author of *Chasing Ghosts, Texas Style*

"An entertaining and interesting fact-filled journey guided by the inimitable voice of raconteur Bloody Mary who brings the dead back to life in her Supernatural guide to the other side of New Orleans."

—Carolyn Long, author of *A New Orleans Voudou Priestess: The Legend and Reality of Marie Laveau* and *Madame Lalaurie: Mistress of the Haunted House*

"I love this book. Bloody Mary brings to life those who are gone but still with us. And Bloody Mary writes their history so beautifully—poetically and lyrically. But, more importantly, she shares her own supernatural insight and experiences with them too."

—Angela Hill, award-winning journalist, veteran news anchor, and New Orleans television personality

"Bloody Mary, Voodoo priestess, folklorist, and storyteller, allows the reader to enter her spiritual and professional world . . . the author illustrates the marriage between the mundane and the spiritual, between the supernatural and the religious, between legends and the truth."

—Alexandra Reuber, PhD, professor of Practice in French at Tulane University in New Orleans

"Fascinating insight through Bloody Mary's eyes into the paranormal and New Orleans. A hauntingly good read."

—Nick Groff, coauthor of *Chasing Spirits* and founding team member of Travel Channel's *Ghost Adventures*

Bloody Mary's Guide to
Hauntings, Horrors,
and Dancing with
the Dead

Bloody Mary's Guide to

Hauntings, Horrors, and Dancing with the Dead

True Stories from the Voodoo Queen of New Orleans

BLOODY MARY

WEISER BOOKS

This edition first published in 2016 by Weiser Books, an imprint of
Red Wheel/Weiser, LLC
With offices at:
65 Parker Street, Suite 7
Newburyport, MA 01950
www.redwheelweiser.com

ISBN: 978-1-57863-566-5
Library of Congress Cataloging-in-Publication Data available upon request

Cover design by Jim Warner
Cover images: Greenwood Cemetery, New Orleans, Louisiana © Paul Souders/World-
    Foto, 6836 16th Ave NE, Sea/Corbis; Sky: Shutterstock © Stephanie Frey
Interior by Deborah Dutton
Typeset in Adobe Caslon Pro

Printed in the United States of America
M&G
10 9 8 7 6 5 4 3 2 1

To all the spirits, especially my mother, Beverly Millan. She taught me how to pray and how to love an undying love—she still does.

Gratitude and thanks also to my living and loving family who ground me here and now, with special honors to Jagger, Matthew, Gina, and Olga.

I am an afterlife coach to those who have passed, but I am always their student. I learn directly from the source— because I listen. I try to help these phantoms evolve and provide a mirror of truth to aid in their rescue, but I believe it is a two-way mirror.

Contents

Foreword

NEW ORLEANS. THE BIG EASY. Like its music and food, the city itself is a blend of cultures, beliefs, flavors, sights, and sounds.

With much of the city residing below sea level, the constant threat of Mother River reminds all who live and visit that life is both fragile and short. Given her history—full of tragedy, travesty, and triumphs—there's no question that New Orleans is America's most haunted metropolis.

In August of 2005, Hurricane Katrina claimed thousands of lives. That disaster is but one chapter in a long book of New Orleans legend, lore, and history.

Around 800 C.E., the Mississippian people settled this region and built earthworks and burial mounds. In the 1690s, the French arrived sowing seeds of their culture that can still be found in every Creole's accent and cooking. Later, New Orleans was caught up in the war between the French and Spanish. The outskirts of town were once full of plantations and African slaves were brought in by the boatload. They brought their folk magic and Voodoo—adding to this gumbo of culture.

Who could forget the infamous early-nineteenth-century pirate Jean Lafitte calling New Orleans his home port? Or Madame Lalaurie, a socialite and serial killer known for torturing and murdering her slaves? With most of the graves in the city cemeteries located above-ground, it's no wonder the dead walk so freely here, including the spirit of the city's most famous Voodoo Queen: Marie Laveau.

What you're holding in your hands right now has been more than twelve centuries in the making. By turning this page, you're embarking on a journey of haunted New Orleans with one of the most visible and qualified guides you'll ever meet . . . Bloody Mary.

Unlike television's ghost hunters who rely on gear and gadgets to look for ghosts, or psychic mediums who offer only their mental impressions of spirits, you have Bloody Mary who blends her psychic abilities with limited technical gear. As a Voodoo Priestess, she can also bring those magical elements into her work. Mary offers drumming and dance, conversation, libation, and of course, creole food, to the spirits as a way to glean a complete picture with local flair.

Bloody Mary is a product of her environment, just as her city is a product of the millions of people who have come and gone through the Big Easy over the centuries. Each person has left their mark on New Orleans . . . and some of those voices still echo today . . . if you know how to listen.

Fortunately, Bloody Mary does in a method she calls Voodoo Paranormal. I've had the privilege of knowing and working with her for over a decade now. I can think of no better person to take you on this trip to haunted N'awlins.

Laissez les bons temps rouler!

—Jeff Belanger, author of *The World's Most Haunted Places*

Preface

WELCOME . . . I AM BLOODY MARY, a born and bred, proud native New Orleanian. My lifelong quest is dedicated to spiritual endeavors the world over, but it is my own backyard that has proved the premier microcosm of mysticism with a heavy hotbed of spirit activity to share. I was exceedingly blessed to be born and raised in America's Most Haunted City, where my roots were planted nearly three hundred years ago, long before we were American. My earliest ancestors Troxler (later Troxclair, or Troslcair), came here from the Alsace–Lorraine area of France in 1718, and their spirits still speak.

Spirits have come to me here since childhood. Throughout my entire life, I've been polishing my understanding of the spirit worlds and how different people entreat them. I believe in angels and saints as the source of many of the apparitions I encounter—they are. I believe in many levels of human and nature spirits, too.

True proof of the supernatural lies in the experience. I share these experiences through a spiritualist and shamanic approach with a cordial bedside manner, and I consider it a privilege and a responsibility for us to work together.

My personal search pointed me to Voodoo some thirty-three years ago, but yours should go wherever makes sense to you. The religion of Voodoo is as cultural here as my native blood, and the spirit world of New Orleans is organically part of it all. Voodoo is a religion that still allows the spirit world to talk to you directly. The ancestors speak; I listen. This is a religion that is alive. It has been speaking to me my whole life, from my own backyard and the waters that surround.

While I am Voodoo, I never gave up my Catholic upbringing. I wouldn't, for it is one with me and my city. My mom was a St. Joseph nun before she married my dad, and I was the result of her ten-year-long novena in request for a daughter. I was trained my whole life, and prior, to pray with the saints as intermediaries. They send me messages and I listen.

I work as a psychopomp but serve as Voodoo Queen. I am also Mamaissi—Priestess of the River, and Haitian Voodoo Mambo Asogwe. I am an especially proud disciple of the spirit of Voodoo Queen Marie Laveau. I preach her tradition, which includes all these aforementioned traditions as natural ingredients in the great gumbo that is New Orleans.

As an earnest and state-sanctioned priestess, I perform hundreds of weddings, baptisms, and death rites—all of which have witness of the living and the dead. I also provide spirit counseling, rituals, and ceremonial healings for the living and the dead. On top of that, I also do house spiritual cleansings, uncrossings, and even full exorcisms, if warranted. But, all in all, people come to me to learn how to connect with spirits more often than to remove them. I teach people how to get along with spirits, clear their own spirit, and conquer their fears.

This treatise is meant to invite you into the other side of New Orleans. Through true story and experience, I hope to help you stop and listen to these Invisibles who still whisper their memories to you before they are silenced or rewritten in the wake. I am their voice.

This book is committed to all those who have come before as well as those who will come ahead who face the danger of losing these precious components of the legacy of New Orleans in these post-Katrina changing times. Join me; let me be your spirit guide, leading you through to the other side of my New Orleans.

Introduction

L IFT THE VEIL WITH ME as we uncover the supernatural world of New Orleans. Hear about the famous and the infamous ghosts of New Orleans in a different light, discover previously unpublished details about New Orleans's most famous spirits—the Voodoo queen Marie Laveau, Jean Lafitte the pirate, our femme fatale Blood Madame Delphine Lalaurie, and Julie, the ghost of forbidden love—and meet some personal everyday spirits that help make this place tick.

Join me for a toast to the ghosts as we travel through portals known and unknown in New Orleans. Meet my spirit mom, Beverly, a few of my personal house spirits, and some phantom hitchhikers that I've picked up though the years. Ghost animals also pop up here and there.

Tag along through New Orleans's cities of the dead. Understand the how-tos of our unique burial process, and get inside-the-box knowledge of what's really hidden underneath it all. Join me as we meet some of the residents I have encountered on my graveyard excursions throughout more than half a century of visits.

See paranormal photos from my ghost photo gallery, then take a walk on the dark side and get details of some of the exorcisms I've been called in to execute. Get behind-the-scenes info on the documented spirit case studies you have seen me cover on hundreds of national documentaries for the past twenty years, and I will even share some case studies never before revealed.

I include a Spirits' Who's Who and explain what they do after each chapter to spotlight specific roles that the dead can help you with. Then, go through to the Afterlife Lessons and Warnings sections to help you understand and navigate communicating with the spirit worlds around us. Discover how-to hints through my personal method of Voodoo Paranormal, psychic connection techniques, and direct spirit revelation.

Come explore the paranormal impact of many of our historic founding families and travel with me all the way up to the impact of Hurricane Katrina. Explore some modern spirit activity accented by my world of paranormal experiences in vignettes through *lagniappes* (that's "a little something extra" in ole New Orleans patois).

I will provide a voice from another era—storyteller prose mixed with modern style with a splash of channeled information sprinkled throughout. The spirits want their stories told. They've even stepped up to correct their own history, and they could jump out of these pages to visit you, too.

I will tell you both sides of the stories I share, and explain the paranormal aftermath still felt today. The nineteenth century is the backbone when many of my main spirits lived in the flesh—these are the spirits who talk the most and are still interested in keeping the old ways present. I have been directly involved in New Orleans twentieth- and twenty-first-century supernatural worlds affairs, where I continue my work as a psychic detective.

The mystic and supernatural side of New Orleans must be realized as just as important to her history as her Creole cuisine, jazz music, and Mardi Gras.

You may wonder why New Orleans is called America's most haunted city. There is never just one answer to that. Wars, plagues, pestilence, and hurricanes have not destroyed New Orleans, and these disasters are not the only things that have created our ghosts. Ghosts are our history; they have tales to tell and recipes to share.

You should also be aware that New Orleans is on great geo-physical ley lines, with portals regularly opening and closing. These dragon lines, faery roads, or ley lines are long-known highways of spirit activity and power grids. New Orleans and Cairo, Egypt are on the same ley line, and when you travel east from New Orleans it shares a ley line with the great tantric center of Lhasa, Tibet. We are the base chakra; we are Malkuth; we are the filter, too. Many things snake their way though our port town by riding on the back of our mother, the Mississippi.

There is also a group of adept ascended spirits here that I call collectively the architects. They have shown me the key to many things and have helped in healing many situations. Their imprint here is deep, and these Old Ones unlock the mysteries.

Believe, or do not believe, in spirits: This is a decision only you can choose to satisfy. I record first-hand experiences from inside the box, from qualitative paranormal field studies, and from the perspective of an avid historian. I simply speak and mark their words and mine. There is a balance and a spirit path embedded here. Power points charged with spirits await if you know where to find them. The spirit of place here is wild and wise. But there is also a dark side . . . Are you ready to look further beyond the veil?

1

Julie, the Ghost of Forbidden Love

I WAS INTERVIEWING SOME PSYCHICS at Bottom of the Cup Tea Room who owned and worked in this known haunted building of 734 Royal Street. Specifically, I was inquiring about their famous resident spirit, Julie. This group shared many ghostly tales: electrical issues, water faucets turning off and on, items disappearing and reappearing, and even one tale about their haunted swing in the courtyard. Everyone had an experience to share—a meandering ghost cat, occasional phantom voices calling them near—plus a unanimous reporting of a very uncomfortable presence. Some reported it as a simple feeling of being watched or "cased out." Words like "danger" and "suffocation" were mentioned. The general consensus was that there was a rather indomitable masculine entity whose darkness was apparent upon occasion. They all agreed that Julie was light and sweet. I was here for Julie at this time, and an important tale presented itself.

A sweet female psychic in her mid-twenties and I exited the main building to the courtyard for our session. Mind you, the entire time we were chatting, I was covered with spirit-formed cold chills that were getting stronger and stronger, pulsating through my whole body. I attributed them to the fact that spirits were near and listening. Doors slammed in the nearby slave quarters, bells tinkled by unseen hands, and soft laughter echoed from the throat of an unseen watcher from the haunted rear patio where we were sitting. My interviewee noticed me trance away ("getting tipsy," as we sometimes say), and laughingly remarked, "Oh, that's just Julie—she's really trying to get your attention." I nodded and bid a kind hello and acknowledged Julie's spirit presence.

The psychic continued, "Once I was napping in this same courtyard, and I was awakened by a beautiful stranger. She was a young woman who appeared barely twenty. She was of olive complexion and very pretty. She shook me to wake me and spoke in a tone of concern. Over and over she repeated, 'Henri Je Rouge, Henri Je Rouge.'"

Mistakenly, this psychic thought the spirit of Julie was looking for someone with that name, perhaps a child. But I knew better, for now Julie had stepped even closer into me, and I was the medium. I knew her real meaning. Plus, as a local, I certainly knew of the feared Je Rouge.

I chimed in, "No, no. She was warning you and waking you to protect you. Je Rouge is a demon—the red-eyed demon, an evil one."

An arctic cold enveloped us from the beyond at the precise moment I repeated that refrain. A sense of urgency was upon me to run out right that minute. This was not out of any sense of fear, just a knowing. Julie was urging me on. It was time to go. The second I stepped out of the boundaries of the building, I realized that the pulsating icy feeling was not a tingling from the haunted courtyard, but was emanating from inside me. Exhilaration is the best word to describe it, coupled with a sense of awe and a sensation that the whole world was my personal oyster.

I began to skip down the street (not a normal pace for me). I even tried to jump up to hit all of the store signs I encountered. Giggling and laughing aloud, I merrily skipped through the Vieux Carré as I was both self and other, overpowered with glee. There was still a slight sense of human embarrassment. Was everyone staring at me? No mind, this felt great! But I had things to do. I needed to fetch my child from pre-K, but that would mean I

Julie's spirit body, with her head tilted, approaching from the left.
Photo by Matthew Pouliot © BMT, Inc.

would have to drive home after. I had to do something to fix this. Then again, I did not want it to stop at all because the feeling was so happy and carefree. There was so much I could learn from Julie, and she from me. I hated for her to leave.

I usually prepare for spirit encounters with protection amulets in hand, but I was empty-handed on this day. No matter, mine were only two blocks away, with sacred altars in wait. I skipped merrily toward the New Orleans Historic Voodoo Museum on Dumaine Street, where I was stationed at the time and where Creole mystic Madame Cocoa was busily preparing her own mojo. I knocked on her door and told her quickly that I was not alone—I had a ghost with me. I hoped she wanted to co-channel and socialize with us, but Cocoa went right to the heart of the matter.

"Do you want me to get rid of it?"

That sounded so final.

"Well, I think I would rather talk and get to know her."

But Cocoa was busy and not in the mood.

"Do you want to get rid of her or not?" she pressed.

I calculated quickly: Pick up child + drive home + cook dinner = "Yes."

Cocoa took her bottle of Florida water from the altar, poured some into her cupped hand, slapped it on my heart chakra, and said "Julie!" The moment she called her name, the spirit was gone. I had not told Cocoa where I had just come from or the name of the ghost.

Julie's spirit was gone quicker than she came, but our connection lingers. I can honestly say that Julie is still a close friend of mine. She was the first spirit to take a full ride on my back that had to be ritually removed. Some nineteen-plus years ago, right at

Orb at a rooftop where the residual energy ghost of Julie walks
Photo by Bloody Mary © BMT, Inc.

my transition from part-time to full-time spirit work, Mademoiselle Julie walked in. She needed a ride.

Her Story

Julie was the most beautiful woman in town: long hair down below her waist, skin the color of café au lait, and eyes of hazel. She wanted nothing more than to marry Zachary in the eyes of God and bear his children. But this simply was not done in the day. Legally, she was a woman of color, and marrying between races was not permitted. She was his placée, a form of legal mistress. Julie did not understand why they should not wed—everyone else in town seemed to want to marry her. Her love for Zachary was beyond compare, as she thought his was for her. What could her one-eighth strain of blood noir possibly mean between their love?

Whenever Zachary was entertaining his friends below, she was expected to spend many a night alone on the third floor. This was a part of his world that she was not privy to, and it saddened her greatly.

When they were alone, they had quite the storybook romance; but these days were few and far between now. For, as in any story-book romance, there was an evil shadow in the background—and this tale has several.

One was Zachary's family. They had selected someone for him to marry—someone of title, someone of wealth. More and more, he would leave his love to spend time with the other woman to appease his family. And more and more, Julie was left alone— trapped, not only by the sadness of her man seeing another woman, but because another evil shadow was weighing heavily on the shoulders of Julie.

Julie was haunted. She saw and felt the menacing presence of the evil spirit Je Rouge. She saw his red eyes in the windows at night. She felt his draining desires. A young lady should not be alone; it simply was not proper. She was easy prey.

And now there was a strange man lurking about. Soon he seemed obsessed with Julie, or possessed. Henri was a local slave, and he terrified her. In Julie's eyes, now he stalked her, too. Now, Henri and Je Rouge were merging as one, and Julie was the one on the menu. It was maddening. She knew not what to do.

When Zachary did come home, all he and Julie did was fight. She begged and pleaded for him to stay, for she truly feared for her life. At first Zachary thought this was a ploy to get him to stay home longer, but soon he realized that this was destroying Julie. Worse, it was destroying their love. Without a word, but with a noble nod, he stared into her hazel eyes, and she knew deep in her heart that he would take care of things. From that night forth, she knew she was safe. It seemed as if all the monsters vanished when he held her in his arms. They never spoke of it again.

Slowly, Julie's strength returned. Her fears subsided, and she was free to deal with the true matter at hand: her man was seeing another woman. No one should marry him but her—it was destiny.

Maybe Marie Laveau would help. She was renowned in the field of love. In fact, she was the mistress of *l'amour*. Her work had an impeccable reputation. So Julie gathered her strength and went to see the Voodoo queen to procure a love ritual. She asked Marie to make their love last for eternity and Mam'zelle Marie gave Julie everything she needed.

With those items in hand, she returned home and climbed up the stairs to wait for her love. The Thursday night card game had rolled 'round, as usual. And, as usual, Julie waited above as Zachary's friends gathered below. But when Zachary climbed the stairs later that night, there was nothing usual about the kiss they shared. It was more passionate than any other. He was speechless when they broke from that embrace, transfixed by her eyes. Why, he couldn't even speak until spoken to. He was under her spell.

The words they shared that night seemed to seal their fate for eternity.

"You have taken care of me in every way for all these years, and somehow you rid me of Je Rouge. You're my knight in shining armor. Now comes the time that I must prove my love back to you," Julie said.

"There is nothing you need prove, my dear," Zachary retorted gallantly.

"It is my debt due," she shrewdly replied, knowing he was foremost a man of honor.

Julie persisted with this demand, and Zachary relented. "Alright then, Julie. If you feel so strongly about this . . . prove your love to me. Walk then. Walk the night on the roof. That will prove your love!"

That night, there was a terrible ice storm.

"If I do that, then you'll certainly marry me," said Julie.

"Why, yes," Zachary said. "In fact, I will marry you in the morning if you walk all night on the roof without the benefit of any of your clothing."

Julie disrobed, much to Zachary's dismay. He thought it would be over and done with, such an obviously preposterous statement. But, then again, he should have known how serious a subject this was with Julie.

"Go. I know how improper it is to keep your friends waiting," Julie urged. "After all, I will be Madame in the morning and never have to leave your side again. But do indulge me. Look deeply into my eyes, the windows of the soul, so you know how much I love you. For I very well could freeze to death up there tonight."

Zachary replied, in all earnestness, "No. My love will keep you warm."

They embraced, and then each went in their opposite directions. Throughout the night, Zachary became increasingly nervous. He did not hear Julie's footsteps overhead as usual. But he was not going to give in to her—not this time. He would find her warm, waiting in bed, and things would be back to the way they should be by morning.

All the night he did fret. At 6 AM, when the cock did crow, Zachary sent his friends away and hurried upstairs to see where Julie was hiding, but could find her not. He raced up to the roof. There, he found her frozen, naked body clutching the chimney. Zachary pried Julie's fingertips from the brick, scooped her up into his strong arms, carried her through the attic window and down the ladder, and laid her on the bed where they once made so much love. The guilt was overwhelming. He had no idea she'd actually go through with such a thing, but he should have known. Zachary held Julie tightly in an embrace until she expired in his arms.

On cold December nights, Julie walks on the rooftop—sometimes searching, sometimes protecting, but most often lingering and listening for love's small *tap, tap, tap* upon her door. Groups gather on Rue Royale waiting to catch a glimpse of what many say is the world's only naked ghost. Most ghosts have more shame, but not Julie. She walks boldly back and forth across the roof in afterlife as she did in life, until the first rays of sunshine hit and she disappears.

Another ghost is sometimes seen: a man, formally dressed in period attire, wandering the rooms. Other times, just his ghostly hands are glimpsed, usually shuffling a deck of cards. And once in a blue moon, two shadow lovers embrace. Sometimes they are even seen strolling hand in hand across the courtyard in midair. For Zachary too died, not long after Julie, they say, of a broken heart.

But there is that other ghost—the dark one. He is the one felt and feared by many who have lived in this building throughout the years. Unbeknownst to me, I was destined not only to befriend Julie, but fate planned for me to deal with this Other as well.

They say that the other side is a mirror image of what happens here; so it seems to be for Julie. For that slave Henri could not rest on the other side without coming back to catch a glimpse of the woman he wanted but society would never let him have. So heavy is his presence that Julie's spirit still feels as though she is being stalked. It important to her to warn people who visit of the evils they may encounter where she once lived. "Henri Je Rouge! Henri Je Rouge!" These are the words I have heard echo from the rooftop. Perhaps she was not really alone on the roof that night.

Séance

You don't have to hold hands 'round a table to have a séance, and you don't have to use EMF meters to have a paranormal investigation; these are really only techy trumpets and bells of modern day that amplify your own psychic abilities.

I cleared permission to do an overnight investigation at 724 Royal Street. My sister Carol, my friend Sarah, and I all collaborate on psychic and spiritual encounters, plus a few fans tagged along. Six women sat to psychically connect.

We were on the second floor of the main building this night. There was a connecting entrance from the slave quarters' rooms to ours and a joint winding stairwell between all the floors. We started with some simple social connections in the parlor, but

Julie's terror and warnings were increasingly felt this night, and Henri came out in all his fury.

It started slowly. We felt there was someone out of place, lurking. Someone who really should not come into the main house; a dark man. The current owner, Glenette, heard the phrase "the bad man."

At one point, I went into a separate room alone to do some automatic writing. The overall message followed suit:

Be careful. Watch out. He is close. Be wary of your company, too.

I said nothing to my companions about this. We continued for another hour or so of mutual channeling and back and forth with our Q&A mediumship. When that social connection part of the night was done (or, more precisely, when the spirits decided it was done), the door to the stairwell slammed shut, sending shivers reverberating clear down to the bones of all. We ran to pursue the culprit and caught the wisps of a white ghostly dress hem as Julie's ghost turned up the winding staircase and retreated to the third floor.

Knocking quickly on the tenant Chris's door, we asked, "Did you see Julie? We followed her to you from downstairs."

Chris and his wife Lisa had many experiences with Julie on countless other nights, especially in the realm of sound. Frequent ghostly dinner parties with the clinking of crystal goblets and murmurs of conversation just out of reach embraced them on many a quiet evening. We all searched for her this night, with no luck. She just disappeared.

Soon everyone exited the building except my sister and I—we stayed overnight on the second floor. We continued our quest and experienced many anomalies, photographed paranormal evidence, heard whisperings through the night, and were followed by the scent of old-fashioned sweet perfume. Later, I had dream visions that were both lucid and concrete.

By morning, I knew how to help. I wanted to do something to protect Julie; my empathy was strong on her case. I gathered classic historic protections against demons, vampires, and/or general *suckeurs*.

I would drive the honey locust thorns into the window ledge that divided the slave quarters from the main house, to prevent Henri from entering and scaring dear Julie again. I treated and activated the hand-gathered thorns with *traiteur* techniques and ole swamp magic. I then whipped up some strong protection oil from a secret recipe. Carol and I then returned to this Royal Street address to seal the entrance.

With our mission accomplished, we readied to leave. As we descended the stairs, I glanced over to the courtyard and encountered an eerie and bizarre sight: Precariously balanced on a narrow brick ledge forming the back wall betwixt the bishop's abode and Julie's home was a young man whom I had seen on many an occasion enter and exit the building. He lived in a slave quarters apartment and seemed to be a quiet man. But on this day, he was a creepy man. He was perched perfectly and was staring at us with an unblinking gaze. His long black coattails were barely grazing that three-story, crumbly mortar and Mississippi mud brick courtyard wall. He appeared sinister, somewhat like a deranged crow stalking prey. He did not move an inch nor say a word. He simply stared with vacant eyes and watched intently as we walked away. Eerie, indeed.

The Red-Eyed Demon

I went back to the Voodoo Museum immediately, where Madame Cocoa came running at me, ready to chastise. Before I said a word, she yelled, "Who have you brought back this time?!"

Uh oh, was I in trouble?

"Come quick, Ms. Mary," Madame Cocoa said, not waiting for my reply. "Come quick. I swear to you—those big red heart bottles you have in the back altar threw themselves across the room all on their own just two minutes ago. Come see."

The broken heart bottles were shattered all over the floor, and I knew who did it. I whispered, "Henri." It must be Henri—after all, the bottles were red. Was his heart broken?

"Who's Henri?" she asked quickly.

"Je Rouge," I said quickly under my breath.

She got angry. "Don't bring no Je Rouge in here! What do you think to bring Je Rouge? I want no part of any damn Je Rouge . . ."

In Julie's day, the Je Rouge was a full-fledged demon, feared as a vampire or sometimes described as an astral werewolf. He had devolved in Cocoa's teenage times to be a less frightening entity and more of a Peeping Tom–type, but he still stalked, particularly young ladies when they were alone. I told Madame Cocoa I would take care of the broken bottles and the Je Rouge, and I did. I gathered all the glass, brought it to the altar, and ritually banished its presence out and away through the red chards of glass. A storm began to brew, and I knew I had gotten through, for I mystically work within storm energy. I left quickly, and though it was difficult to drive, I made it home with my child in tow and quickly shut the door on the storm.

Nightfall was now upon us, and maybe something else, too. Settling in, I noticed my son Jagger was fixated, staring in trance at the backyard. My little whirling dervish toddler was quite the spirit seer, but he was rarely still. The storm was rough, and the flashes of lightning focused their glow upon a plastic jack-o'-lantern that had somehow flown out of the yard and attached itself to a high spot on the garage door, now framed ever-so-perfectly in view of my child's back bedroom window. "Oh God, he followed us. And of course he's trying to frighten us, too."

He did provide quite the Hollywood horror setting that night. I decided I'd best sleep close to my son, for his sake. Just in case. Henri was obviously angry. I had awakened that Je Rouge within.

Then the phone rang. It was Sarah, and she was frantic. "Someone—something followed me home, and now my scissors are missing. I was just using them. I walked to the other room and came back and they are gone! I've looked everywhere." The storm was raging, accenting her story and perfectly punctuating the fear in her voice. It was no fleshy form of which we spoke.

"Calm down, calm down," I said. "It's going on here, too. I'll take care of it. Just go to sleep and trust me."

Sarah was no stranger to the spirit world. She was a natural medium, but young and untrained. She was also my responsibility. I promised to have a little heart-to-heart with Henri and send a veil of protection remotely around her. Calmed by my promise, Sarah went to sleep. Healing is accepted more easily when the person is calm and receptive.

I set to work. I knew I could appeal to Henri's humanness and get rid of his Je Rouge. First, I explained Julie's fears to Henri, and, whether warranted or not, I told him that if he truly loved her, he would not want her to be afraid. After all, his intentions were never clear to her. It was that fear, not him, that drained Julie in life and was still scaring her now. His obsession was unhealthy. It made room for darkness to seep into him while he was alive, and it had now been with him for more than a hundred and fifty years. I reminded Henri of his own mother's pure love and some of the simple things from his life that would make him smile. I also let him know how society has changed (somewhat). I was sorry that he had experienced unrequited love and racial injustice. He seemed to understand. His intensity softened as I spoke. He then left. The storm went with him.

Sarah called in the morning. "I found them. The scissors were under the cushion of the sofa I fell asleep on and in an opened position. They were not there last night!"

"Interesting! You know, open scissors are used to cut the path of haints, *cauchemar*, and other boogeymen," I said.

"Really?"

"Yes, I actually have a pair of open scissors on my altar now."

Sarah was protected that night.

My sister Carol was also followed home. She felt disconcerted, as though a menacing presence were watching her. It affected her so much, she slept with the lights on for days on end. She never normally does such things. But in our family home, where Carol still lives, both of us had grown up with suspicious entities lurking about. Neither of us was a stranger to this plight.

The protections around my home door and my guardians were strong and held in place this night. Henri only stayed near the back entrance of my abode and did not get in. My son always insisted on sleeping with full lights on, and so it was that night.

The incident did not scare me. I simply did what I had to do. But for the case of the ghost love triangle on Royal Street, I still connect with Julie. I know that Henri never meant Julie any harm. He just loved her so. He would do anything to catch a glimpse of her—even in death. But fear is a brutal bed partner, and Je Rouge still terrifies Julie.

Does the Je Rouge still attack? Perhaps. That strange young tenant, the seemingly meek and mild man watching us from a narrow brick ledge of the courtyard that day, was ripe for the pickin' and right in the line of fire.

It seemed that when we saw him perched so dangerously on that ledge, watching us like a hawk, Je Rouge was already moving in. Or perhaps he had been connected to Je Rouge all along. I am unsure. Shortly after we saw him, the man moved out. He had to. He was found climbing naked on the roof—the same roof that Julie walked that fateful night so long ago. It was said to be a suicide attempt.

Or could that be just one of the many strange coincidences found in the annals of the repeating history of the Vieux Carré? If you believe in coincidence.

On December nights, when freezing temperatures reach their lows, the beautiful ghost of Julie paces the roof and balcony of her home on Rue Royale. An early nineteenth-century ice storm may have claimed her life, but not her spirit.

The Spirits' Who's Who

- **Je Rouge**—This vampiric entity is one of many *suckeurs* seeking sustenance from the living. He has the capability to possess a human form and can tap the life force of his prey through the physical or astral realms.

- **Matchmaker**—Julie is a ghost of love. If you have love needs, she likes to try to help. She wants to see love flourish. It makes both her and the world a happier place. This may have always been her life's mission, or it may have emerged from the lessons she learned during her particular life, but her job is matchmaker. Write Julie a letter on yellow paper with blue ink and give her a slice of coconut cake and she will help you find love.

- **Shade**—A ghost of the netherworld. This is the classic definition of a ghost gone rogue—a mere reflection of the spirit that once was—like Henri's ghost who still stalked Julie in the afterlife. Henri provides a mirror, reflecting how we trap ourselves in situations and revealing how this can drain our soul. Henri was trapped in a loop and needed a reminder of the man he once was so he could let go and ascend to his full spirit self.

- **Walk-In**—Spirits may sometimes step into humans to communicate with you or to feel through you. This can happen for countlesss reasons: through invitation, ritual calling, message relay, boredom, curiosity, or even attraction. Sometimes it happens because of simple proximity. Voodoo calls this medium the horse—ridden by spirit.

✦

Afterlife Lessons

I feared that if I had cleansed Julie away on our first encounter that I might lose our connection—an incorrect and naïve passing thought of twenty years ago. A connection can always be there. But they can't all move in with you—there just isn't enough space.

I was aware that I was not alone that night and was lucky to find the source quickly so it did not root in. We all pick up things in life, through our associates and the places we travel. You don't have to be on a ghost hunt for that to happen.

Don't expect this all to be easy. My life built a way to blend it all together, choreographed with the spirits themselves. It is a beautiful dance, but some of the steps were really difficult to master and balance. There were tests that felt like they could tear me apart. There was a lot of jealousy aimed toward me along the way, and some sadness and darkness, too. But it was balanced by the beautiful wonder of it all, and all in all, every step made me stronger. I also made some spirit friends along the way, like Julie who taught me the benefit of long-lasting spirit relationships.

Angry does not mean evil. Henri's anger—smashing bottles and trying to scare us—were signs he was just mad. No one listened to Henri's side, ever—only Julie's side. Once Henri's story came out, his anger subsided. After all, he was cut off from seeing

Julie in his human life, and I had somewhat caused the same thing again by installing entrance protection blocks.

I banished that Je Rouge demon who had possessed Henri more than a hundred and fifty years ago. This attachment stuck to Henri's soul and forced him to be stuck as a mere ghost of his former self. When I blocked Henri that night, it triggered a memory of his human self. Anger was the first response, but I won him over by triggering the memory of love and helped his broken heart beat again. I spoke to Henri gently and firmly and released his Je Rouge.

Warnings

Not all walk-ins are as sweet as Julie, and not all people can balance between worlds while holding on to themselves. Don't try this at home just for fun. I am rather strong at balancing between the worlds since I am a psychopomp (Greek for "guide of souls"). This refers to a person or spirit who helps humans transition to the other side as well as souls transition to the human side.

Beware of walk-ins. Beware of the Je Rouge. Just be aware. Keep clear.

The dark side lurks and strikes faster when our energy is low. When we are emotionally weak or sick, things can stalk us more easily and latch on tightly without struggle.

Unhealthy obsessions in life must be put in check, for you could carry the darkness with you, etched onto your soul into the afterlife. Clean out your closets regularly while you are alive so that you are clear. Do not fear the dark side, for we will face it in life. Just pull yourself together and balance.

Bring gifts for the spirits and grounding tools for yourself.

Always open and close gates consistently. Opening and closing gates is not summoning forth unwitting or unwilling spirits from the depths. It is putting a protective sub-circle within a circle that exists naturally. This provides a structure for easier communication with resident spirits who are already there.

Opening gates by specifically stating your intentions to the spirit world then giving a gift in the process for socializing, and closing the gates with thanks when finished are polite and proper protocols. This is for greater communication and ensuring protection for all when we end.

Cleanse, rinse, and repeat.

Lagniappe

Hitchhikers and
My Haunted House

SOON AFTER MOVING to my home in 1999, my son came running into the room, bleary eyed, to complain: "Mommy, make them go away."

"Who, honey?" I asked.

"The ghosts."

"Which one?"

"All of them."

"Are they hurting you?"

"No, they won't let me sleep. They're dancing about my room, singing and laughing. I can't sleep."

"How many? What do they look like?"

"I don't know. Some are in costume—women, men, kids—lots of them, Ma. Just tell them to go away. I don't want them living here with us anymore."

"Okay, Sweetie. I'll take care of it. Sleep in my room."

I was quite used to having an entourage follow me—after all, it was my job. I was never fearful or worried about these things, but I guess it was a full house. I soon realized the importance of taking charge of these situations sooner rather than later. As a strong, protective single mother first and foremost, I kept my son's well-being as my main concern. There was really no time to negotiate.

I'd need to tend my altars, pray, address the spirits, and gather the necessary herbs and tools. First, I opened the gates in a protective way and stated my intention clearly as I anointed the candles and set the lights. I prayed to gather strength, then married the components with my mortar and pestle and called the herb's inner spirits forth. I also called on my own spirit protectors, guardian angels, resident house spirits, and patron saints. I acquired the anointed iron cauldron to hold the working and burned the copal-and-dragon's-blood mixture that created the remedy to "Send Back." With words of power, I went to all the openings and began to smudge this sacred smoke at every window, door, crack, and crevice that I could find. I whooshed away the marauders with my sacred rattle and horsehair whip. So, with a stern "You don't have to go home, but you can't stay here" last call, I did my priestly and motherly duties and cleaned house.

I followed up by mopping with ammonia, which is a simple and effective remedy for spiritual cleansing. I always add brick dust to my mop water too to bring in the good and to protect.

I did what I had to do to make my child at peace, and then I tried to go to sleep. But I wasn't done. All through the night was the rat-a-tat spirit rapping at my windowpane; a full-bodied symphony of metal-to-glass tapping in a seven-count beat at thirty-two-plus entrances, windows, doors, and transoms. It was as if four or more spirits were stationed at each entrance with pennies in hand, tapping in unison for eight full hours. They wanted in and were diligent in their process. Had it not been for my child's request, I would have let them back in and just said, "Okay, but behave. I'm tired."

But instead, it was, "Sorry. No. I have to protect my child's needs. You just can't live here." It was just too much or too many. I told them I would see them again on my journeys. I was firm but polite. After all, they were not evil, just a bit bothersome. I felt bad, but I held my ground for the entire eight hours of attempts at reentry until they retreated.

Success! All was quiet for some time. Banishing complete.

Weeks later, however, Jagger came running to me again. A very strong and hard-to-open attic door and accompanying folding stairway crept open with a resounding *cree-eee-eek* all by itself, which sent my child rushing to report.

"The attic! Mom, now they're coming through the attic!"

"Damn! I forgot to cleanse the attic."

I cleansed the whole house when our interdimensional overload proved too cluttered, but I'd neglected the attic. The attic had always been active and noisy, but it was out of sight and out of mind. Now, I'd best climb up and fix that quick. I would anoint the four corners of the attic door with holy oil so the spirits would not intrude upon Jagger that way again. A mother's work is never done!

I directed this particular banishing to the hitchhikers, not the resident spirits—they have visitation rights. And from then on, I set my boundaries more clearly with my spirit family and residents in my haunted home.

I still invite those hitchhiker spirits that I evicted long ago to birthday parties, graduations, and even occasional TV shows, but the invitation clearly states when the party's over! Boundaries are important, balanced with respect and social interaction with the many dimensions we coexist in. Many of those hitchhikers that moved into my home long ago were just lonely. I let them know that I would see them again, but they couldn't live here.

My house is listed in Jeff Belanger's *Encyclopedia of Haunted Places* and has been featured on major television shows, including *Ghost Adventures*. My ghosts scared the hell out of the *Ghost Adventures* boys, and I found Nick and Aaron sitting on my front

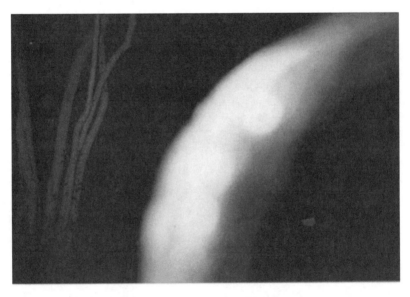

Arc of orbs or vortex in Bloody Mary's front yard
Photo by Bloody Mary © BMT, Inc.

porch after only an hour of investigation, waiting for me to escort them back inside. My ghosts threw books at them, hissed, cursed, and rushed them out the door. I cordially and formally opened the gates that night and then I left the *Ghost Adventures* boys home alone. I called the four directions and opened the gates in a ritually trained and official way, addressed the spirits of place, and then there was a voice from the sidelines that chimed in, breaking protocol. It was Nick, calling, "and the malevolent ones, too!" They called the dark; and they got what they asked for. But when they left, not a creature was stirring, not even a . . .

Even with boundaries in place, spirits can still make their opinions loud and clear. They certainly stepped in during our recent renovations, and my spirits were not shy at all about their total disapproval of a previous boyfriend—and it turns out the ghosts were right. They also did not like the *Ghost Adventures* crew when they came to investigate, either. I think they were looked at as intruders. On the other hand, they tolerate my husband and have learned to love him, too. And I understand. My ghosts are definitely hard on men, and they can be overprotective.

Here are a few of my guidelines to keep in mind as you're creating your own rules of the house:

- Don't wake me unless it is important.

- Do not hurt or scare my friends.

- Stop hiding things. (We're working on that one.)

- Protect us.

- Kick anybody's ass that breaks in or has ill intentions.

(Boundaries may need to be revisited and reset.)

Edouard and Thomas are protectors of the house and the family. They shared the role as male head of the house when I first moved here as a single mom. They still protect and guard us from intruders to this day.

Edouard particularly protects the house itself during renovations. Edouard was the original builder. He's a thin man with light brown hair pulled back in a little ponytail, and he shows himself in a thick humanoid presence in the kitchen, back hall, and front entryway. He acquired this property in 1894. He always shows up when someone new, especially workers (particularly men), are nearby.

Thomas is a soldier and a fierce protector of Jagger and me. He hated my ex-boyfriend and caused all kinds of ruckus when he came into the house. Thomas also hated when I left town to visit this ex during our long-distance relationship. The stomping of Thomas's loud, heavy boots, smashing of items, and slamming of doors were heard by downstairs neighbors whenever I went out of town, and the aftermath was left for me to clean up upon my return.

I have about a dozen house spirits, a ghost dog, constant poltergeist activity, and a haunted collection on top of that. Some items in my haunted collection were gifted to me, some were ancestrally inherited, and some were intentionally gathered. I have immortelles, spirit bottles, and many acquisitions. They also get tender care and are not "bound" here.

Bloody Mary and her snake, Dani Blanc, in the main temple
Photo by Sabree Hill

So my house came with spirits, I took some of my work home with me, and as a psychic medium and mambo I have a hierarchy of spirits that come and go during my rituals and healing sessions. My home is also my House (my Voodoo temple) where we have a Voodoo family tradition with my husband, son, co-priestess, and other godchildren.

My son and I are both very psychic. My house knew this when it called us. All in all, Jagger has dealt with the spirit world his whole life and is not afraid in the least. He has a beautiful view of auras, and I have always taught and encouraged his confidence in his own spirit strength. He's a natural healer who came into this world with immense knowledge about the other side. Countless hours of his tellings and guided meditative journeys taken together have reinforced both of our strengths and nurtured our spirit protectors.

✦

The Spirits' Who's Who

- **Family Guardian**—Spirit family members who guard their loved ones may come to visit at different times with messages or warnings. They also provide strength when times are tough. My mother, Beverly, is a welcome and important guardian. My God-family and friends also fall into this the category. So do my house spirits, Edouard and Thomas.

- **Foster Child**—A spirit child who visits regularly but is not a full-time resident. Ariel is a little girl around three or four years old who is my adopted hitchhiker. She used to hide things around the house a lot until I acknowledged her and got her some toys of her own. She particularly likes her Little Mermaid doll and children's tea set. On occasion, Ariel will bring a friend and they play together. The toys sometimes move by themselves. Though things still go missing and reappear, I no longer credit just her. Many spirits do that seemingly for no reason, but maybe they're using the missing items for a spell on the other side.

- **Ghost Animal**—The spirits of animals who guard or visit people or places. Butch is our ghost watchdog. I had a houseful of rescue ghost animals after Hurricane Katrina, and Butch may be a remnant of those days or he may have lived on the premises in the past. He was not my previous pet. He comes and goes, but he definitely guards the house and can be fierce when necessary. He manifests and acts just like any pet, though he's heard and felt more than he's seen.

- **Hitchhiker**—This is an uninvited spirit or ghost who tags along and follows you. I have had many hitchhikers over the years. When I'm tired or busy and I forget my regular grounding routine, they may slip by. Visitors may also bring hitchhikers with them. Some visit temporarily, some are just lost and lonely, and some could be troublemakers. I have had all types over the years, but it's important to keep it in balance.

- **Spirit Doll**—Some dolls become housing for a spirit. Haunted living dolls, which move, talk, or even walk, are thought to exist because they are hollow: There is a vacancy waiting to be filled. Several of my dolls came with spirits; others had spirits step in after I'd acquired them. I also make surrogate dolls imbedded with spirit from the get-go, usually for the specific purposes of healing, guarding, and such.

- **Spirit Guide**—Guardian angels, celestial beings, saints, Voodoo Loa, or met-tets (patron Voodoo spirits of the head), and ascended masters are all subcategories of spirit guides. Marie Laveau, the architects, my met-tets, and patron saints are some of my many spirit guides. (I will continue to be a spirit guide when I cross.)

- **Spirit of Place**—A spiritual life force of a house or land. The spirit of place beckoned me in and showed me my new home. There was no FOR RENT sign—just the beautiful, faded nymph statue in the backyard fountain. While I was driving by one day, her head turned toward me as I was pondering where to move when a bad situation had arisen in my current apartment that threatened my young son.

- **Trickster or Bully**—Many spirits can have a trickster side to them. These spirits can also be serious helpers and tricksters combined. (I am.) Tricksters can teach you a needed lesson though chaos, and this may be their higher purpose. Spirits are teachers, but they can also be true practical jokers, though at times it seems impractical or inconvenient to us.

  You need to determine whether the spirits around you are just bullies or whether they knock you on your ass because it's the only way to get a lesson through to you. Bullies are immature or insecure entities that are mainly interested in pushing people (or spirits) around. They run when it gets real, and they try to set up others to take the fall for their misdeeds. Bullies are troublemakers that manifest poltergeist phenomena or otherwise cause disruption and thrive on the attention. Do not feed this cycle; ignore it or laugh at it until it balances. Then help them, if they let you.

- **Visiting Ghost**—Sometimes spirit guides or ancestor spirits that traveled with a human visitor choose to linger and stay behind. Many may be present temporarily during and after a client's psychic or healing session. They may also assist in continued work for a client afterward or be in need of transformation work themselves.

- **Watcher**—A watcher is a spirit who guards a space. Ilene is the female motherly energy who is seen and watches my house from the front porch and main entrance hallway areas. Ilene was the first ghost/spirit I encountered when I moved in. She lived here just prior to me. She is about five feet tall and has been seen in broad daylight with shoulder-length gray hair. One woman whose grandma lived here prior to me encountered Ilene many times. On Halloween, neighborhood children have seen her on the porch, where she guards the candy.

Afterlife Lessons

Trust and believe your children. Listen to them without judgment, and guide their spirit connections. Remember, the young are close to the spirit realms from which they came. They were born with knowledge, and it fades as they age. Marvel in all their wonders. It is a natural ability. Let them ground and instill that they have power over their own lives. Teach them how to use it, not abuse it. One of the worst things to tell your children is that they are crazy or demonic if they demonstrate psychic abilities. This is normal and natural.

Acknowledge the helpful nature of your house spirits, and pay compliments along with the boundaries you need to set. Negotiate your house rules and set up your protections.

There are doors that paranormal people are opening and summoning through, even if they think they are just doors to battery compartments on their electronic recording devices. There are also older keys pressed in time, passed down though the ages to open and close doors more safely that one can learn to use instead of just bursting through doors without merit and walking away leaving gaping tears.

This is all summoning spirits; it is real. Proper ritual training teaches to open gates through a gatekeeper/crossroads spirit's intervention, and this is a more protected way to travel to and fro. They hold these old keys. Many psychics and ghost hunters feel that it is their job to push ghosts to cross over quickly, assuming that ghosts have not tested those waters and cannot swim freely through them. Others command and provoke spirits. Both can be doing a disservice. Only a very few are "stuck," but all of them (and us) are readying for further ascension prior to the next journey.

✦

Warnings

We all walk through things every day, and we can track it with us, leaving our mess behind. Some carry way more baggage than others. We never walk alone. Wipe your feet when you come in the door. In fact, putting something under the doormat to absorb and cleanse all who walk through your door is smart. Salt is a quick fix—keep sea salt around.

Be careful during renovations. That tends to wake up the ghosts more than anything else. Remember that to the spirits it may look like you are destroying their property. I suggest telling the spirits your plans *before* you start. Ask for their advice, and even lay out the blueprints. You never know—an idea that pops into your head may be one they sent. If the spirits disagree, explain the situation again, perhaps adding a glass of wine to the mix.

Careful what you ask for! Don't invoke malevolent spirits; there's enough stuff we step into accidently in the world to invite any extra! And if you do ask for such, be ready to own it and take your just desserts. Scapegoating is self-serving and self-abating.

Do not jump on the Evil bandwagon; this just feeds fear and calls darkness near. Aggressive or outwardly active spirits do not mean evil. Fears are self-consuming. Elevate your own spirit.

2

The Voodoo Museum, Seven Ghosts and Counting

I TOSSED AND TURNED IN THE NIGHT and rolled over to snuggle with my son. As I cuddled him close, I felt the familiar hug of a two-year-old boy reaching out to his mother. His soft, sweet caress filled me with instant warmth and love as I embraced him with reciprocal attention. I readjusted the pillows a little and came to the realization that my son was eight now and I am not even at home. Opening my eyes fully, I saw that I was embracing a cherubic blond little boy whom I did not recognize. I was sleeping in my Voodoo parlor in a slave quarters apartment behind the main building of the Voodoo Museum.

He was such a sweet-looking boy, and though he was not my son, I was indeed a caring and concerned mother. But wait! Was he really an innocent child, or was he in disguise? It didn't feel like he was putting on a show, but I was with knowledge that occasionally spirits take on an innocent facade to gain your trust. I sat up and asked, "What's your name?"

He did not reply—perhaps because of his age or a language barrier? I asked again. Still no answer. In remorse, I replied firmly, "You're not my son. I need to know who you are. Show yourself."

His full flesh manifestation instantly melted into a spirit shade, and the once gorgeous, cherubic, full-faced, healthy baby turned gaunt. His body withered to a sickly, frail frame. The skin paled yellow as he lifted out of the bed and began to fade away. The once-soft curls framing his perfect features flattened and lay limp, drenched with sweat. Perspiration beaded on every pore of his body as he reached out to me in desperation with his weak, lanky arms and cried in agony that wrenched at my heartstrings, attached to the sadness that I could not relieve his pain or his fear. He seemed to pull away farther and farther as I reached out for his sweet embrace in vain.

I projected all the love a mother could give, and the boy quickly and quietly disappeared through the wall. I prayed with all my might and continue to cry out, "Je t'aime! Je t'aime!" hoping the French words of love were familiar to his ears and that he could still hear me as he journeyed on his way. I realized that this precious little boy was but one of the tens of thousands who were claimed by that demon Yellow Jack in the plague that besieged New Orleans for so many centuries.

But this particular child died in my arms, as he must have died in this building so long ago. I tried to comfort him on his journey and was deeply saddened by the loss and all the pain mothers feel, not only at the time when this town had the highest infant mortality rate in the country, but by all mothers' losses across time. It was an overwhelming sadness and empathy. I shed many tears that night and sent sympathy and solace to all those who feel that loss, to help them hopefully recover, as well as to help that one specific beautiful little boy on his way. His cries and reaching arms haunted me for some time.

This place had lots of ghosts, but I had not encountered this boy before or since. I continued to pray and mediate his journey. I carried him in my astral arms to deliver him to a safe place, to his angel mom and caretakers who were awaiting him on the other side.

Had he been here all this time, waiting, or did he just reach out to a living mother who could help him on that particular night? I don't know the whys of that night or what specific trigger summoned him to cuddle in my arms, nor does it matter, for all I believe and hope for is that I helped him.

That was an odd night for me and a deeply emotional one filled with serious spirit work. Each step and each encounter teaches more and more, if you let it in.

Trickster Tom and the Hungry Haint

The most regular spirit visitor in that slave quarters behind the museum main building was a trickster fellow. He had a penchant for hiding things, particularly panties and cigarettes. The few friends I let stay there concurred with me that those items consistently went missing. One time, panties were taken right out of a packed suitcase without disturbing a single other thing.

Oil painting of Marie Laveau by Charles Gandolfo that hangs
in the New Orleans Historic Voodoo Museum
Courtesy of New Orleans Historic Voodoo Museum

Occasionally, the packs of cigarettes would turn up on chandeliers and microwaves and the like, but the panties never came back. We called him Tom because he definitely peeped.

But before I met Tom, something else was lurking there, something not so nice. And it was hungry. It seemed to just hang around waiting to sup on the next victim's energy that moved in. I watched the tenants' energy drain away one by one. One even came out feet first!

I knew I had to shoo it away or I might be next on the list.

I needed to do a very big banishing on the negative energy lurking within before I moved my spirit realm there in 1999. And I was exceedingly careful in the cleansing ceremony and very specific on where I set up my altars afterward, too. I placed talismans and imbedded Voodoo protection symbols known as ve-ves at strategic points to prevent any evil from ever returning

That hungry ghost was meticulously banished away in stages. First, the burning of heavy-duty shaman's amber tears to expose the culprit, followed by several strenuous swamp magic curse-reverse rituals. Then that darkness finally cleared. That thing was really more than just a single ghost; it was more of what we call a haint—a collective force. I do not really know how it got there or why it was there. I do know that much life and death has occurred in that brick townhouse since its 1835 beginning, and maybe it finally collected together and needed to feed.

Le Collections

We have all heard about haunted museums. Previously owned artifacts in museums or antique shops could have residual attachments from previous use, a bloodprint, or even a full-fledged ghost tagging along. Multiply those beliefs one-hundred-fold when you are talking about acquiring ritual occult items off of unknown dead persons' altars and putting them in a collection. Perhaps the items could be incongruent with each other, or they might have questionable spells embedded in them. Most of the time, the collector is unaware of what kinds of work were done on the collected pieces. I have been in the Voodoo Museum alone and with groups of patrons when certain pieces just came to life just by my pointing to them and talking about them. Occasionally, some have not just fallen down, but flung themselves across the room. I became very diligent about feeding and opening and closing gates, but not everyone was.

Founded by artist-curator Charles Gandolfo in 1971, the Voodoo Museum is a dusty old collection of Voodoo and Hoodoo artifacts from New Orleans and southeastern Louisiana. The Voodoo display room consists of a wide variety of Voodoo dolls, gris-gris charm bags, statues, skulls and bones, dusts, and lots o' jujus, too.

The Voodoo hallway is filled with a hand-painted collection of Voodoo practitioner portraits, most created by the curator, affectionately known as Voodoo Charlie. Charlie became a Voodoo practitioner during his own anthropological dig for the root of New Orleans Voodoo. In many ways, his work has him acting the avatar of Papa Lebas, our own Voodoo gatekeeper and divine messenger.

The Primo art display is the quintessential portrait of Voodoo Queen Marie Laveau. Charlie honored and loved the spirit and the woman. And Marie's spirit emanates hauntingly and literally through her portrait. There is also a splintered section of wood from Marie Laveau's kneeling bench and a wishing stump carved from the old tree at her famous wishing spot at Bayou St. John, where Marie Laveau's adherents faithfully call her spirit.

The altar room is filled with displays dedicated to New Orleans Voodoo, specific spirit/loas, and previous queens and kings. Some have been activated through prayer, petitions, and offerings made by countless visitors throughout the years. It is in here that the snake spirits are greatly venerated. The great mother and father spirits—the serpent and the rainbow, Damballa and Ayida Wedo—are leaders in the pantheon. The great ancestral god La

Grande Zombi is our Great Ancient Venerated One and the Patron of New Orleans Voodoo, also depicted by the snake. Mami Wata, or Maman You, is of utmost importance and is perceived as half human, half snake or mermaid.

Ghost Snake: La Grande Zombi

One night, as I was cleansing altars in my parlor, I was compelled to stop and go out to the courtyard, where I saw a serpentine apparition floating near the back corner of the garden. I was lured closer to the reptilian spirit with surrounding feu follet ghost lights when—*Poof!*—it disappeared. I took this as a sign. I looked down and knew I had to dig, so I did.

Lo and behold, I uncovered a curse: It was a map of the French Quarter with a burnt effigy around the address of the Voodoo Museum—a silly revenge spell put on the museum by a disgruntled ex-employee. This person was a fly-by-night drifter who wandered into town and made contact with an online Hoodoo worker who sold spell classes on the Internet to anyone who would pay her fee. I guess apprenticeship with in-house, step-by-step advancement was not quick enough for this one-armed bandit's misguided goals.

I was rather angered by this discovery and did a hex reversal, Johnny-on-the-spot. La Grande Zombi and his full feu follet kin pointed me to this mis-spell, and I mirrored it back full force so it would misfire and be destroyed. The spirit of place booted the ex-employee's tired ass right out of town. I guess her spell did work, but bass ackward.

Courtyard
Photo by Bloody Mary © BMT, Inc.

Ya know, if ya got the gift and the spirit partners working with you at your side, secrets are revealed to thwart misdeeds. That snake spirit showed me that spell, and about two years later an actual one-hundred-pound python named Zombi was buried in that exact spot.

Ghost Gator: Le Grande Crocodille

There are also many bones and skulls—human and otherwise—in the Cemetery portion of the main display room. Many are just bones, but some are more. In this area, it is the gator man who has the most tricks up his sleeve. He is a fully dressed, life-size, moss-stuffed, gator-skull-topped effigy sporting full long sleeves—a juju theriomorph par excellence. He is propped up here, watching. Working with this great protector spirit of the swamp, technically called upon as Le Grande Crocodille, there is really nothing tricky about him—his is deep chthonic and ancient work. But this specific gator man manifestation living in the museum has developed a distinct personality and sense of humor. He is like a big, gator-headed, scarecrow-esque Voodoo doll. He is *not* empty inside and *is* embedded with spirit. Occasionally, he turns his head all by himself. I've caught him, and so have others. Recently, a customer was taking photos in the museum, and for no reason at all, the photo of gator man and the nearby cemetery altar came out perfectly upside down. Constant trails of orbs and ectoplasm appear around his body in some photos that I've taken, while others never come out at all.

Gator man display at the New Orleans Historic Voodoo Museum
Courtesy of New Orleans Historic Voodoo Museum

Ghost Cat: Le Chat Noir

There is indeed a ghost cat, and he probably emanates from his great and powerful juju—the petrified black cat. He used to rub up against my leg and follow me around the museum (the ghost cat, not the petrified one). I have seen him dart about the courtyard and inside the old slave quarters rooms. In his juju form, he is quite awesome and fearful—a perfect deterrent. In Voodoo, this acts as his "grotesque" kin in France that dons the cathedral spires: the roosting guard gargoyle. In this case, he is a bit more like cat jerky than stone, dangling overhead in the Voodoo display room. His familiar phantom form has manifested to me sweetly on many a night.

The dreaded black-cat juju was a powerful totem to ward off evil spirits. There was a lot of big bad Black Cat Hoodoo going on around nineteenth-century New Orleans Voodoo.

Animal spirits are quite common, the familiar and the strange. Theriomorphic types and maybe, just maybe, some juju, gris-gris, and mojo are in store for you, too.

Voodoo Charlie's Ghost

The founder of the Voodoo Museum, Charles Gandolfo, died on Mardi Gras 2001. I planned and presided at his Voodoo ritual funeral in Congo Square. There was a large turnout. Priestess Miriam and I both got "hit" with Voodoo Charlie's spirit. He definitely came to his own funeral, and his spirit was happy. I wrote in his eulogy that, in a way, for man with a longstanding New

Black-cat juju display at the New Orleans Historic Voodoo Museum
Courtesy of New Orleans Historic Voodoo Museum

Orleans Creole lineage such as Voodoo Charlie's, Carnival was an appropriate day to die. He was definitely proud of his Creole heritage—and he still is. His spirit pops up now and again at my house, at mutual friends' homes, and at his Voodoo Museum.

Voodoo Charlie loved the ladies, but he used to be more of a gentleman. When I take groups to the museum at night now, if a pretty girl is close to the shutters, she might get a pinch on the bottom or feel touched, which is just Charlie letting himself be known.

There is a silent memorial to Charles Gandolfo in the museum, where his ashes and his favorite chapeau are displayed. His spirit guards the area, as he has a strong connection to his collection.

With the recent passing of museum employee Dr. John T. Martin came an end to the physical snakes in the Voodoo Museum. Docent and snake handler Dr. John T. is now in his own heaven tending to the ghost snakes that always live in spirit at the museum.

Since that major ritual undertaking in 1998, nothing dark has returned. Spirits still roam around the museum, and some of the altars and artifacts could awaken any moment, when the right triggers (or the wrong ones) come near.

The museum building came with its spirits. Some additional spirits came along with the collections, and maybe even a few more followed me in. No matter their source, there is spirit in the Voodoo Museum.

✦

The Spirits' Who's Who

- **Altar Spirit**—This is a spirit imbedded in the altar itself and/ or in an individual altar item. Fetishes, Voodoo dolls, roots, gris-gris, jujus, totems, statues, masks, portraits, crosses, and countless other spiritual items are more prone to come with these occult attachments. They become magnetic conduits and could carry both the altar spirits invoked through them and the essence of the actual practitioners who created them. These items could be spelled and enchanted intentionally to house a particular spirit as a form of reservoir, or they could be imbued with spirit simply by the nature of serving at these altars consistently.

- **Attachment Spirit**—This type of spirit is commonly found as a display item in museums, private collections, and antique shops. These items need not be works of art, and they could actually be quite mundane items that are quite precious on a personal level, such that a spirit will not let go of them.

- **Curator**—There are spirits who are overseers of collections in shops and museums. Voodoo Charlie acquired a collection, created the concept for the Voodoo Museum, and was a hands-on manager. He was a curator there in life, and so mote it be for his afterlife.

- **Feu follet**—This is a local swamp spirit, also known as flashing fire, fools' fire, faery light, ghost fire, or will-o'-the-wisp. This blinking ball of light is known to lead you to treasure or water and to lead you astray, mostly in the forest. Here, it led me to a buried spell in the courtyard.

- **Haint**—For anyone who dies quickly or abruptly, his or her soul is in shock and can get stuck here on our plane. Most will meander toward their kindred kind in the swamps, and there, these spirits coagulate into a mass entity called a haint that reeks of slime and moss. It will jump out and attack you and suck your life force, like a psychic vampire. A haint may hover and feed before it is strong enough to travel on.

- **Juju**—This is the spirit of sticks and stones and black-cat bones, gator heads and "dem bones of de human dead." The animistic beliefs of Voodoo have spirit and an inherent power or medicine within their remains. Like the relic bone of the saint and the Catholic belief that a saint's intercessory power is in every fiber of their physical remains, so be it in Voodoo. Voodoo beliefs go further and include animals, certain trees, bodies of water, stones, and more. So our black cat and gator man are these reliquaries (aka jujus). Human bones, ashes, and personal artifacts of past Kings, Queens, and practitioners in the museum are jujus, too.

- **Resident Spirit**—This is a spirit who visits their old home in spirit form. They can be children, adults, and even pets. Past owners of affiliated businesses or even a trickster or two can show up as well. In this case, all types!

✦

Afterlife Lessons

I believe it is always important to cleanse any new place you move into. Set your boundaries, state your intentions aloud, and introduce yourself. This will make the space your own.

I recommend that you befriend the house spirits and respect those who came before you, but take care of any squatters who intrude.

Pay attention to your collections. Make sure you psychically feel out each item to determine if it is a match for you and for the other pieces in the collection.

Address the spirit of a lost child, especially your own, even if you never carried them to term. Pray for their spirit. Thank them for choosing you. Apologize for not being able to fulfill your role for whatever reason, and name them. You can help guide them to a safe haven so they do not have to wait for others to do so.

✦

Warnings

Camera anomalies happen in the Voodoo Museum on a regular basis, as well as on many of my personal outings to haunted and sacred sites. I advise all to ask permission of the spirits prior to taking pictures or there could be repercussions. To give an offering of food, liquid, or coins to the realm is even better. I preach respect and social graces to all life forms. I have a friendly bedside manner as long as the spirits do. They need energy to manifest, and the first thing that goes is the batteries; a gift of something else to feed on prior resolves about 90 percent of these issues.

Spells are a dime a dozen. Good, solid morality should be established before teaching any student who comes knocking (or clicking). Discipline and discernment are being forgotten in our instant-gratification age.

Cleansing of residual energy is warranted on people, places, and things. Look at it like a stain—the sooner you cleanse it, before it sets in, the better. Some stains are more damaging than others, and not every stain reacts well to the same solvent. Sage is not the universal solvent. There needs to be an element of psychic diagnosis first, then an execution of the task. I use Florida water or salt and camphor or copal, and, for stubborn cases, asafetida.

All metaphysical/occult objects should be treated properly before adding them to your collection, and extra special attention should be paid to weaponry or items with a bloodprint.

Occasionally, something sinister could wear the suit of a child to lure you in. Ask them directly if they are actually a human child ghost or spirit. Do insist on seeing their real form, and try to get their real name. There is power in the name.

Lagniappe

Angel Mom, My Longest Love

M Y SON AND I CROUCHED down in the hall as I rum-
maged through the closet to help him find a flashy
evening gown. The echo of complaint from hubby
Matthew surrounded us in the background:

"What? How could a high school promote a transgender day?"

"It's no big deal," Jagger replied.

"I'm going to make it fun," I said.

"OMG, you can pull off a great Rita Hayworth look with that
hair!" I exclaimed.

My sixteen-year-old son rolled his eyes in response. He had
no idea who Rita Hayworth was. This was perfect, because my
son Jagger has hair that is long, full of perfect ringlets, and carries
a deep, rich auburn hue. He had never needed to borrow a dress
before, but I have a huge collection of fabulous diva attire.

"Yeah! I hit the jackpot!" I'd found the perfect one. I began to help Jagger slip into this skin-tight, low-back, gold-sequined, full-length gown of perfection, with its mink-fur-trimmed cuffs and hem. The moment he was all glammed up, a little hurricane hand-cranked radio/flashlight hidden away on a nearby junk table began to play. Somehow it wound itself up and perfectly tuned itself to a station playing a traditional jazzy stripper song. That radio rarely worked and never tuned in well to any channels when it did. It also hadn't been cranked up by human hands in years.

Jagger and I looked at each other and laughed, tears welling up in both our eyes as we said, "Hi, Grandma. We miss you." (At this time, my mom had been deceased for about a year.) My mother's spirit surrounds me. Beverly visits both my home and my sister Carol at the old family home. For me, my mother's main messages come through music. She loved to dance, and sometimes songs play out from hidden and somewhat defunct radios, stereos, computers, and music boxes when she is coming through. Even in her aged days in hospice, the happiest times for her were when music played. Her eyes danced on even when her legs could not. They lit up just like a little girl.

The other happiest times were when my mother was near babies.

I received a Facebook message with a message from Mom, a reminder call around Easter 2014. One of my mom's hospice nurses from four years prior had tracked me down. She said my mother's spirit had been coming to her for the past five days. It was good to know Mom could still get around.

She explained how my mom had also communicated messages to her from her own deceased mother when she tended to Beverly

Bloody Mary's ancestral altar with photo of a young Beverly
Photo by Bloody Mary © BMT, Inc.

in hospice. The nurse said my mom knew things only she and a very few close family members were privy to. She also confessed how Beverly would be under the covers talking to the angels when she checked in on her.

She didn't know why Mom had come to her now, after all this time, and she had to find me to figure it out. During our conversation, the nurse began to talk to me about my being a medium and felt comfortable enough to share the psychic connections she felt with those dying in her care. She told me that most of her patients waited until she was on shift to die in her arms. It was very sweet. She was there when my mom took her last breath. I thanked her and told her how important her gift was.

Toward the end of our conversation, she confided that an old friend of hers had died recently and had visited her in a dream. She was unaware of the friend's passing when the vision came. She took the prompt and eventually gave her friend a call earlier that day, right before we spoke. When she called to reconnect with her friend, that's when she found that she had passed the Friday prior.

"Well, there's the link," I said.

"What do you mean?" she asked.

"You said my mom started to come to you five days ago, which was Friday. My mom was helping your friend come through to you. Sometimes other spirits have to be escorts, for they have the strength and experience that the recently passed ones may not have mastered. My mom remembered your kindness and was helping your friend get in touch with you."

"Oh, it all makes sense now. I knew I had to find you!"

The hospice worker had not put those things together. She thanked me and asked me to tell my sister Carol hello. I called Carol to update her about Mom's new role on the other side.

Carol reminded me that God had told Mom that she was going to be assigned to take care of babies who had passed. I had forgotten about that, though I don't know how. She is my personal spirit mom and an angel mom on the other side to many children. It's definitely a job made in heaven for her, for as I mentioned, my mom *loves* babies. I also reminded Carol that when Mom was young, she worked for the telephone company as a switchboard operator, connecting people together then, too.

Out of the blue one day, a psychic informed me that my mom was watching over my baby. I had miscarried on April 11, 2005.

Very few people were aware of that loss. My mom has protective and guiding roles on both sides. I thank her again for all the love she gives.

The Spirits' Who's Who

- **Angel Mom**—Spirits assigned the role of taking care of the young that die, especially the babies. They nurture them and help them grow and make sure the little ones are safe and loved on the other side. These are usually different from spirit moms, who watch over their own children. My mom is both. Beverly is a conduit of grace and wisdom for her family here and takes care of other children in need on the other side.

- **Escort**—Friends or family members who are already on the other side who come to assist the newly dead on their journey. Some spirits are stronger and more suited for this task than others. My mom helped the nurse's friend in this way.

- **Messenger Spirit**—A spokesperson who helps spirits send goodbyes or messages to the living. Sometimes the newly deceased sender is not developed enough to send a strong enough signal on their own or the human receiver does not understand the attempts. My mother in life gave messages to her hospice nurse from her deceased family. My mom in her afterlife was also trying to help that same nurse recognize her own talents—Facebook helped, too.

Afterlife Lessons

Music is the universal language. It crosses all barriers and dimensions. I play music for the spirits, and some even play a little music for me. Sometimes signs are subtle, so it's important to stay in tune.

All the senses are able to connect to the other side, so pay attention to all of them, but focus on your strongest sense first and begin to develop from there instead of reaching for gifts that are further out of reach. Work with what you have, and the other senses will fold in naturally. Trying too hard to connect can block you, for it is best to be in a receptive, relaxed state for the flow to grow.

If you are developing your spirit connections, try sending visualizations for communication, drawing a picture, or even writing a letter to the other side. Talk, sing, play music—whatever works best for you. You have to practice with each partner to help your particular dance go smoothly. This is true with the living and dead.

My mom's hospice nurse has beautiful psychic gifts that she is slowly developing. A new one may be to help others find their way, besides those who literally die in her arms. My mom was trying to help the nurse recognize her talents. She prompted that nurse to find me so I could validate her. Her fellow nurses do not share her sentiments, so my mom wanted to let her hear how important her role is and to thank her for acting on it.

Every person who passes can use a death midwife to help them along. I told my mom stories and was with her before and after she crossed over. I saw her spirit separate from her body, starting with her ghostly arm gliding up and out through her solar plexus with her index finger pointing upward to heaven hours before she died. Three days after her death, right at her cremation time, I traveled right ahead of her spirit and watched the gates open automatically for her. A breathtaking soft, living cloud of light rolled toward the gates. It was mesmerizing and not at all like the glaring bright light in the movies. There really was a gate, but no fence!

Remember that all your ancestors are still your family. This includes those ancestors not yet born, for their spirits may already be with you. Some children are born before their time, or have temporary visas of sorts and choose you. Cherish your moments together and remember them often. Name them, pray for them, and perhaps play music for them, too. These things can help their journey and yours. Even if it has been years, it is never too late.

Warnings

Trust your gut, and do not let those less intuitive than you shoot you down. Whether plain skepticism, religious upbringing, or scientific logic guides their motivations, simply smile and nod at the naysayers and continue to connect. Polish the gifts God gives you.

The untimely death of the young is devastating for parents. Expunge any guilt for your own healing's sake and mourn, but do not despair for your children's well-being. They are being taken care of by angel moms.

3

Madame Lalaurie, La Vampyra

I WATCH INTENTLY AS A SHADOW crawls across the side balcony of this old Royal Street townhouse and disappears. A smaller shadow on the mansard roof above peers over the top of this French Empire–style mansion and dissolves into a wake of orbs that dance on another level of rooftop nearby. The curtains on the exquisite French doors pull back on their own and something watches me watching it from within this tainted house on the corner of Governor Nicholls Street. Maniacal cackles echo from an empty room of the downstairs parlor when I am sure no one was living there at the time . . . not in the flesh.

Dark shadows move freely inside and out to the courtyard. Inside, a freshly made bed shows the outline of a person sinking in, and warmth radiates from a body that simply isn't there. Electronics go haywire and many doors open and close on their own as phantom footsteps approach. An unidentified substance only slightly thicker than tears has been rolling down the walls for the past two years. No leaks, pipes, or physical source is ever found to explain it. These ectoplasmic drips ruin exquisitely painted walls again and again.

This house may have never been without spirits. Even as it was being built, previous residents may have already been on the property—underneath, in the ground. Skeletons found on the site nearly a hundred years later were thought by some to be older than the 1831 house itself.

The prison hospital graveyard on the old Ursuline convent property was only five houses down. It spread closer to Madame's property as death ravaged New Orleans. The records are not detailed year by year, but the graveyard's perimeters expanded over time, and over time there was just more death. Miasma was feared to spread from corpses; if spread, it would eventually claim the innocents nearby to add to their ranks. The Ursuline nuns on this old convent grounds knew of this concern, as did the city herself, as all the cemeteries' dead crept closer to the living. These "evil fogs" were thought alive with death, so this miasma was not to be taken lightly. The nuns left for many reasons; they disinterred their dead nuns but took no prisoners. The grounds were then sold off, lot by lot. This is where the Lalaurie mansion was born.

Torturous Truths

It all started in 1831, when Madame Marie Delphine de Macarty Lalaurie fancied a home on Rue Royale. She quickly pursued this desire and purchased the townhouse from Emilee Troxclair Soniat and Edmund Soniat Duffoset. Young Emilee, my cousin, received these lands as dowry, and a luxurious townhouse for herself and her new husband was underway. Though the townhouse was to be their new home, Emilee perhaps felt something was not quite right, for she did not take up residence there. Instead, she wisely chose to sell the mansion, perhaps escaping a terrible fate.

So it was actually Delphine de Macarty Lalaurie who took residence first, along with her third husband, Dr. Louis Lalaurie, four children from previous marriages, and the Lalaurie toddler. To Madame Lalaurie, it was a perfect townhouse. The mansion was one of the first with gas lighting, of French Empire style, and lavish to behold.

Delphine's eldest child was already half her age, in her early twenties, as was Delphine's new French physician husband; but no one in the house had a spark of the vitality that Madame did at age forty-five. Delphine's new young prey was easily lured into her widow's web, entrapped by her expert grace, seductively woven with wit and experience. All this was strengthened ever more by her love potion–perfumed silken purse, conjured with the strongest of pheromones: wealth, beauty, and power. Louis was putty in her hands.

Soon Delphine and Louis's new home was filled with many a soirée, ball, and masque, and everyone wanted to attend. Even some Americans were invited, for political or financial reasons of course. (The Americans and the Creoles did not get along.) The lavish parties soon ran rampant with rumors of marital squabbles and mistreatment by Madame of her slaves. It was also noted that Madame would sit at the table, looking oh-so-bored, and excuse herself with a feeble comment of checking on the cook. From afar, one could hear the lash of a whip and faint screams. Madame would then return to the party, a bit excited, a touch sweaty, and continue with the meal as if nothing had happened.

Formal complaints were made, but the local authorities succumbed to the power and incessant charms of the irresistible Delphine. Her maiden Macarty name was of an important and well-connected founding family, and she in her own right was a quite accomplished woman of her day.

Yet the Americans would still take these tales to the government—in those days a government run by wealthy Creoles. These native-borns were outraged by the idea of anyone daring to besmirch the name of a Creole, especially one as beautiful and charming as Madame, who couldn't possibly harm a fly, much less a human.

Madame, in many ways, remained above reproach. Yet rumors of the lash of the whip and emaciated slaves spread from the gray stone walls of her forty-room mansion dominating the corner of Rue Royale and Hospital Street. She was not feeding her servants or taking care of them properly. She never let them attend the Sunday Voodoo dances at Congo Plains with the other slaves. All this was against the law.

Since the source of many of the rumors was the Americans, they were disregarded as envy, at least at first, though it was common knowledge that white Creole women were especially harsh on their servants. Still, this case was chalked up to jealousy. That thought pattern persisted until something was witnessed at the side of the house. Then even the Creoles began to change their tune.

A neighbor heard screams and looked outside to see Madame chasing a young servant girl around the age of eight with a bloodied whip in her hand. The chase crossed the courtyard, up flights of stairs, in and out of the rooms. The screaming grew louder, and the beatings harder. The chase ensued all the way to the roof where Delphine viciously beat the girl down, down into the eaves of the roof. The neighbor covered her eyes in disgrace, wanting to see no more . . .

She may have covered her eyes, but not her ears, and she was startled by a powerful thump.

Turning back just in time, the neighbor caught a glimpse—a flash of Madame flying down the stairs, bending quickly to pick up the waif who was totally limp, as if every bone were broken, and hurrying to hide her in the house. Then, "by the light of a torch, a shallow grave was dug in the courtyard later, in the middle of that night," reports Harriet Martineau in her book *Retrospect of Western Travel.*

This story was told, and now people not only listened, they also felt a twinge of shock, and then shame. Rumors and whispers broadened: Did she fall? Was she pushed?

The neighbor witness made formal complaint, and it seems that Madame was heavily fined. Her six or so slaves were confiscated, but no criminal charges were filed. Townsfolk said that she had the slaves secretly returned, bought back at auction by other family members. No longer could these particular slaves be seen in the light of day in her presence. This was not the first time Madame was accused of "barbarous treatment" of her slaves, and the talk of the town was that the upper garret of the servants' wing was a prison to many of them.

Wildfire rumors became arson fact, as a fire broke out in the outside kitchen of the mansion in 1834. It wasn't until this fateful day of April 10 that they could pin anything on her, though it still remains a subject of great controversy. Once this proverbial Pandora's box opened, it continued spewing its dark denizens for more than 180 years and counting. For those who were not on the scene that day, all the newspapers in town plus a few national publications detailed the scene in print for them to verify, and of course countless eyewitnesses spread the word directly.

It was during a small dinner party that the fire broke out. Many went to the source, to the outside kitchen, only to find that an aged cook deliberately set fire to the house rather than live in her condition any longer. She was chained to the wall and fireplace with hardly any slack of chain. The townsfolk broke the chain and got her out to safety. But it seemed that the entire town had assembled—like moths to a flame—as fire had destroyed so much of their city before. The cook told tales of how she had been chained up for over a year and that others inside were in much worse condition than she. Now the Creoles were incensed. This sort of thing was not supposed to happen here. Not with our liberal slave laws. Not in La Nouvelle Orléans.

Dr. Lalaurie arrived on the scene but offered no assistance in checking on the safety on any of the servants within when asked. A reliable eyewitness, the notable Judge Jean-Francois Canoge, was smugly advised to mind his own affairs when he offered official aid to the young doctor. More crowds gathered.

A volunteer fire department entered the scene and got the flames under control. It was not that large of a fire. It never made it to the main house, but with the excuse of looking for burning embers, firemen began to search the rest of the house. From room to room they searched, until they found one barricaded in the garret of the slaves' wing and forced entry. They got more than they bargained for . . .

A visual nightmare and a horrid stench greeted their entry and permeated the room. At first they were taken aback by this fetor of death, but they soon realized that most within were still alive. Alive perhaps just to be tortured longer, but alive nonetheless. They passed a crude experimental-type table with blood-encrusted devices upon it. Glass jars lined the shelves, some of which had human organs inside. The whole sight was a "horrid display of twisted and tortured slaves, emaciated and wild-eyed with fear."

The April 11, 1834 edition of *The Bee* reported:

> Seven slaves more or less horribly mutilated were seen suspended by the neck with their limbs stretched, [and] were torn from one extremity to another . . . The slaves were the property of the demon in the shape of a woman . . . Language is powerless and inadequate to give proper conception to the horror which a scene like this must have inspired.

Armand Salliard, the French consul, reports to the Foreign Minster of Affairs in 1834:

> [Delphine] condemned her servants to dreadful torments: blows, wounds, tortures, deprivation of food. I never saw

more of a horrible spectacle … dislocated heads, the legs torn by chains, the bodies streaked from head to toe with whiplashes and sharp instruments … When the slaves were discovered they were already devoured by maggots.

Jeanne deLavigne's investigative reporting into this dramatic torture scene compounds the horror as her sources claim, that the room had doglike cages stacked upon each other containing humans. One was surrounded by buckets of the prisoner's own blood with her limbs protruding. Another, when removed from her cage, appeared more crab-like than human—horribly atrophied. Yet another appeared to have a face like a gargoyle's. A large, naked male slave was cowering in a corner. He had been castrated, but on closer examination it appeared he had been a victim of a crude sex-change operation. Another slave was found with parts of her skull peeled back to expose "worm infested disease areas." French Council Salliard and *The Bee* added, "Many blacks now ashen gray, shackled with iron collars and spikes and tortuous instruments too confusing to describe."

All of these slaves were brought out that day, one by one. Now an angry mob was brewing—torches ablaze, nooses in hand—and they blocked the nearby docks to prevent Madame's escape.

But it was too late. Delphine gathered her valuables and escaped with the aid of her trusty butler, her coachman Bastien, who also was said to be her spy. They concocted a plan for going out as if nothing were awry—a normal evening drive. Bastien readied the carriage and assisted Madame into her chariot and the crowd mysteriously parted the way for her highness. They did not truly even try to stop her! Slowly they trotted down the street. By the time the shock of her audacity had slipped away, the angry crowd began to chase, but it was too late. The carriage burst through the crowd as Bastien cracked the whip in exquisite fury and escaped with Madame out of the Vieux Carré, down Bayou Road, and all the way out to Lake Pontchartrain. There, a schooner was secured to get her safely across the lake to the town of Mandeville, where she readied legal documents and arranged passage to Paris from New York's port. She lived the rest of her years in Paris, never to return to La Nouvelle Orléans (alive, at least) again.

The day after the fire and Madame's great escape, more newspaper reports emerged: The *Louisiana Reporter* said, "Digging up the yard, bodies have been disinterred . . . bodies were underneath in her yard . . ." A child's skeleton was found in the well. This further infuriated the public. The crowd lashed back at her domain. Since true justice had been cheated, and Madame was gone, the house was to blame.

More than $40,000 of damage commenced over the next few days. Windows shattered as if by a tempest's hand. An angry lot hurled streams of smashed chandelier tears. Contorted piano keys snarled and bound with strings of steel gave an offbeat chime accented by the precious ping of crystal stemware ricocheting off Madame's fine china. All together, this helter-skelter symphony chipped and chirped as witnesses dodged the darting debris, watching it shatter and stake deeply in the heart of the earthen streets below. The citizens' anger and humiliation were vented upon this looming house of gray until it reflected the true soul of what it once hid. The mob vengefully repainted the mansion its perfect shade of Dorian Gray.

To the outraged citizens perpetrating these deeds, it was more than just the pain and horror of the once-hidden scene within. It was also the lies, the humiliation, and the shame. Destroying the scene of the crime might erase the horror, but it did not. The house lay in a monstrous state—open, empty, gaping, and festering the poison within, for years and years and years.

Death's Toll

In the eighteen years leading up to this fire, we know that Delphine owned at least fifty-two slaves. At least eighteen slaves are still unaccounted for. We know that a few survived—several were sold and one was freed. But twenty-four total were verified dead since she donned her second set of widow's weeds, plus the seven that were rescued from the fire that day who seem to have died at the Cabildo (city hall) shortly thereafter.

Delphine never understood why she could not return to her beloved New Orleans and pined for home during her years in Paris. Her own son, Paulin Blanque, verified certain truths about his mother in letters from France:

> Time has not changed anything in that indomitable nature, and that by her character she is again preparing many sufferings . . . I bemoan . . . the fate that awaits us if ever again my mother steps foot in that place [New Orleans], where her conduct elicited general disapproval . . . where she goes we prepare ourselves for bad news. I truly believe my mother never had any idea concerning her departure from New Orleans.

Madame needed tough-love persuasion from her family to abort her constant return-trip desires: "Don't let the fear of displeasing her [Delphine] make you recoil from what you will have to say about the impossibility of her return . . ." emphasizes Paulin.

Death tolls' debt paid its due December 9, 1849 with Delphine's demise. On her dying bed, Delphine sought solace in the fact that her body would be shipped home to New Orleans. Thirteen long months after Delphine's death, she patiently lay in wait for this voyage, bidding her time in the catacomb of the Notta and Noel families at Montmartre Cemetery in Paris. On January 7, 1851, her dream to return to New Orleans was fulfilled. Finally she was en route to reclaim her native soil.

Oral history tells us that Delphine was laid to (un)rest in a family tomb in St. Louis Cemetery No. 1. Perhaps Madame's son Paulin built that large six-shelf family tomb to receive the prodigal "Madame de la cassette" not so fresh from France, but recent interment records provided no documented proof of any interments there before 1884. New Orleans newspapers from 1851 and 1852 do, however, report Delphine's return.

In 2011, I searched for Delphine's spirit in Paris. I visited where she lived and died, and where her funeral was held. I also spent a week at her temporary tomb in Montmartre Cemetery. I was made very aware of Madame's spirit lurking in Montmartre, as she was of mine. She also made many sufferings for me in the process, and at least one miserable sleepless night accompanied by a complete and unexplained power outage at the Ibis Hotel overlooking her grave. I suppose I had to earn my right of inquiry and pay my own toll. I found that modern Parisians and Delphine's contemporaries were both aware of her story.

Madame's cause of death remains a mystery. It was reportedly due to a wild boar attack during a hunt in Pau, France. In 2003, I decided to explore that region myself and found Madame's spirit, but I did not find any historic hunting accident records. Death certificates in Paris list no cause of death in general, so none was listed for Madame. Was it a wound or infection from this alleged hunting accident? Or did she die peacefully in her sleep from a lingering illness, as others suggest?

I've discovered a rather telling and obscure lingering illness for Madame. Family oral history passed Delphine's blood disease theory to me many moons ago, but I have finally found a written record corroborated by Pierre Ebeyer in his odd book, *Paramours of the Creoles*. Pierre claims his mother reports Delphine's demise was due to "perspiring blood." This is a rare disease called hematidrosis, where a human sweats blood. It can ooze from the forehead, nails, umbilicus, and other skin surfaces, causing nosebleeds, bloody tears, and spontaneous menstruation. Even today, in some parts of the world, those afflicted are thought to be victims of an evil spell, or to have a supernatural origin. Hematidrosis is also triggered by fear and acute anxiety. Victims are especially noted as being hysteric women.

Madame's well-known eccentricity was noted by family and friends in Paris as explanation of her reputation. The March 13, 1892 edition of the *Daily Picayune* put it this way: "her high ungovernable temper . . . almost border[ed] on insanity."

Was this Madame's personal "hysteric stigmata" affliction, a "pseudo-sanguineoa," or "ghost spell"? Medical treatment for hemophilia-type afflictions in Delphine's day was indeed drinking actual blood, a much-rumored pastime of our dear Delphine. However, the question still lingers, did she or didn't she partake?

Somewhere in the vicinity of New Orleans there remains a coffin with the remains of Madame Lalaurie in it, and with it lie many, many secrets.

Ghosts of the Lalaurie Mansion

The first and most commonly reported ghost was the little slave girl, falling over and over in a spiraling demise to the bottom of the courtyard. Reports of her plunging death had police on a wild goose chase, leading them to stop answering calls. I have seen the little girl often myself, and previous tenants have seen this wraith within the rambling rooms and skipping merrily on the colonnades.

Nonetheless, as time went by, the house on Rue Royale filled again with many businesses and lodgings: some unaware, lured by the cheap rent, others who thought they could capitalize on the horrors, and many in-betweens who seem to have had their stays short and not so sweet.

Sicilians moved into the mansion and it turned into a tenement house of horror—animals butchered by unseen hands, twins and their mother terrorized by a white-robed wraith, naked Negro slaves in chains attacking residents on the stairs. They did not stay long.

One night a man woke to an angry but beautiful phantom choking him violently in his sleep. A different dark shadow spirit came to his rescue and pried Madame away, and he watched as the ghosts retreated and disappeared through the wall. This man escaped with the aid of this benevolent ghost only to find two gaping, bloody holes gashed in his neck, blood still pumping, and he fainted on the spot.

No one stayed long in that house through much of the nineteenth and early twentieth centuries. A shopkeeper went mad in a single night within the oppressive gray walls, and when he was found in the morning, he never uttered a word. He did not have to, for the stock spoke for itself; it was covered with human waste and putrid filth.

Portrait of Lalaurie (oil on canvas). Reprinted from *Madame Lalaurie, Mistress of the Haunted House,* by Carolyn Morrow Long, University Press of Florida, 2012.

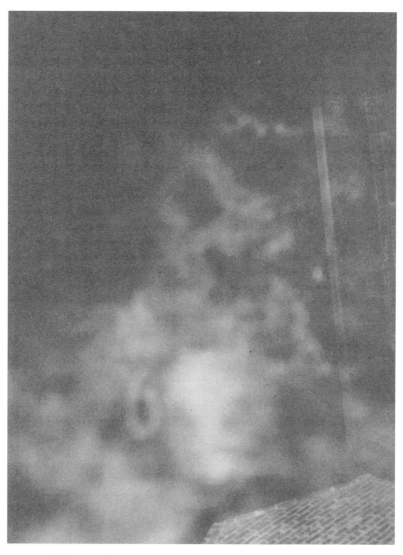

Madame Lalaurie's ectoplasmic head, with empty eye sockets and
open mouth, hovering above us
Photo by Bloody Mary © BMT, Inc.

Later owner Fortunato Greco thought he could capitalize on the ghosts and ran a haunted saloon called the Haunted Exchange for sixteen years. But the ghosts got too real for him in the end.

As time marches on, many private owners have moved in—most all with anomalous tales to tell or tragic endings to boot. Various reports of both denial and declaration of hauntings within the house in modern times come forth from tenants, and a general blockade by subsequent owners to invite investigators in has not stopped the spirits from letting themselves be seen, felt, and heard. Sightings from the 1830s to today continue, of course with the star, Madame herself, taking bows to the thousands—sometimes peering through the curtains or looming over the rooftops, and other times following guests in and out of the rooms, and occasionally all the way home. I ritually open and close gates now as part of any excursion to prevent this type of thing, and carry Florida water with me for a quick fix.

It is the domineering, controlling Delphine that most people see, yet her other face, the one of longing and fear, occasionally manifests. Otherworldly music echoes from within the walls around Christmastime, and the sounds of forgotten children playing confuse occupants through the years. Neighbors report seeing odd things in the slave quarters and courtyard below. At times I have encountered several spirit slaves—some frightened, some strong, like Bastien, her coachman. Not only do masters and slaves walk those rooms, but later residents, now deceased, still visit this haunted house and perhaps a few phantoms from before it was even built.

There are consistent reports of paranormal occurrences, visual and audiovisual, accumulating. In solitude I have been given glimpses of many sordid things that went on within those walls through vision and retrocognition, remote viewing, and automatic writing.

Major renovations have altered the face of this imposing gray mansion throughout its years. An early 1922 renovation seems to have unearthed seven skeletons in or near an abandoned well. Many believed that those skeletons predated Madame's residence, but others said absolutely not. Regardless of when or where the skeletons were found, this was before forensic science, so we will never know how old they actually were, or at whose hand they fell. They were removed from the site.

Tales of construction crews uncovering skeletons in closets permeate New Orleans's history. Stray cadavers in courtyards are the landscaper's norm. And outside known historic cemetery boundaries, forgotten coffins often thwart construction. Most neighborhoods built on top of old cemeteries in town actually do *not* report any extra paranormal activity, but the Lalaurie mansion at 1140 Royal Street may be an exception. The historic Ursuline convent prison hospital graveyard is cited on a map of the 1946 Louisiana Historical Quarterly as being on the same side of the street as Madame's mansion, five houses down, extending toward her property. The cemeteries did expand rapidly because death here had a voracious appetite. New Orleans did build over old graveyards often without moving all of the bodies.

Of course, Madame's story has been told thousands of times throughout the years, and it is often exaggerated; the tortures become more gruesome and the ghost stories more plentiful. Stories have been printed since 1836 and were whispered by eyewitnesses long before then.

Modern-Day Happenings

A Hollywood Connection

Of the many people who've taken guardianship of the Lalaurie mansion, one very famous owner of the ghost house on Royal Street stands out: actor Nicolas Cage.

People say Cage never slept one night in his house of horrors, but that is simply not true. After all, it was his home, and it is a commonly known fact that he loves New Orleans. He was certainly familiar with the tales of the Lalaurie mansion when he purchased the house in December 2006. He also purchased the adjoining house next door. He could be seen coming and going from both, morning and night. Cage was friendly to the people on the streets—he waved and spoke to us from his haunted balcony. It seemed that, as far as he was concerned, he loved his house in spite of its past and did not show any fear. According to Tommy Williams, the caretaker of the mansion for Mr. Cage, "It was Nicolas's favorite home, and he intended [for] it to be his permanent home."

Unfortunately, the house was foreclosed on November 12, 2009, due to a steady string of bad luck and accounting issues. Was this Nicholas's fated bad hand dealt by phantom hands, or just life's card-shark style? Maybe Madame did not want to share the limelight, or the house needed to be vacant for a while to regroup. Who can say? What we do know is that the Lalaurie mansion has been on the auction block many, many times before, and Cage still plans on being a very permanent resident of New Orleans one day. He built himself a beautiful pyramid tomb in St. Louis Cemetery No. 1.

Renovations

After the foreclosure, that house lay still through much of 2010, empty of life. Even then, I heard the shrieking of maniacal laughter in the middle of the night from inside those walls. The house was discreetly sold by Regions Bank to Texas millionaire Michael Whalen under Whale Nola LLC in July 2010 for a song—just $2.1 million dollars.

Renovation would come in spurts. Talking to the construction workers during the renovations, it seems they were all very much aware that they were not alone in the house. There was a sort of occult overseer keeping their work in check. No catastrophes or Hollywood horrors were reported, just an uneasy feeling of being watched.

However, one of the house electricians confessed to one very peculiar anomaly: "The original chandeliers were taken down and boxed and were stored in the attic for a whole year while the house was rewired. We opened the boxes to reinstall them and they were already brightly lit! No normal electrical power source did that!" This occurred in March 2011. That's a hell of a lot of electromagnetic energy, but it seemed a sign of approval! The house was ready to reopen.

Renovations on the incredible 11,000-square-foot mansion may have opened some old wounds to stir its already bubbling brew. Renovations usually do! It laid near dormant for about a year, and still now is seldom filled with life. Michael Whalen does not live there as a permanent resident. The house is presently used for occasional parties or to house guests, and it seems to be just one in a medley of mansions for millionaire Whalen, though probably the only haunted one.

Tommy Williams continued to work on the Lalaurie premises for Whalen until his death in 2012. (We miss ya, Tommy! RIP.) Now Tommy's wife, Carol, continues that legacy at the mansion and care-takes with her family, various assistants, and a string of decorators. She continues to report ongoing paranormal occurrences, as in this October 23, 2013 interview with *Times-Picayune* reporter Chris Granger:

> There's also the sound of footsteps when no one is home. "I can hear them in my apartment," she said. "It sounds like it's coming from the third floor."
>
> And there's the weird thing with the phones. The house's land line likes to dial Williams' cell phone—all on its own, again when no one is home . . .
>
> "I feel very comfortable here," [Carol Williams] said, but then paused. There was that one recent incident.
>
> Williams was at home with a friend on a Tuesday night when, suddenly, the microwave in her apartment came on, her front door flew open, the TV starting playing, and her dog, a Yorkie, began barking on high alert in the direction of the bedroom. He couldn't be quieted.
>
> "Then my cell phone rang," Williams said. "I didn't answer it. We just got out of there.

An Insider's Incident

Cindy Badinger, designer, artist, and owner of the French Quarter's Gallery Nine Forty, is a frequent insider at the Lalaurie mansion. She called on me to get a grip on an anomalous incident inside the property in early 2014.

"Mary, I was on the little balcony on the side of the slaves' quarters when I noticed a caterpillar on the ficus. I went to get the hose to spray it away when a large, black shadow figure crossed my path," Cindy said.

Cindy is no stranger to paranormal activity within those walls, so she chalked it up to one of the mansion's many ghosts. "I got the hose, turned it on, and walked across the courtyard to spray the plant. Then I jumped. A tremendous bang, like a gunshot, hurt my ears. I turned, and the hose was completely severed and water was flowing from the middle. What could do that?"

I inquired immediately. An intense pressure on a hose's center might cause a buildup for such a backfire explosion. But nothing was there in the flesh to produce the tremendous weight necessary to induce this reaction—nothing of weight on the physical plane, at least. The weather was not extremely hot or cold. The hose was new. Paranormal photos taken of the property at this time revealed a gargoyle-esque figure in the forefront and a white angelic apparition in the background.

Was the motive of that particular shadow person an act of dramatic recognition or a show of power? Was it one of Lalaurie's three slave gardeners, Thom, George, or William? Cindy did not ask and was not afraid, but she was perplexed.

Paranormal experiences constantly occur in that house, and Cindy does not feed any fear into them. She also does not feel any danger. Her closet and her spirit are clear. Her position in the house is understood and welcomed. She is safe, and so are most, but absolutely *not all*.

Did miasma mold its own demonic haint, dressed in fine silks and brocade, to become the true evil in this tale? Or was it the deeds within these walls that beckoned evil near to sustain it with the bloodlust frenzy freely overflowing from within? You be the judge.

Not Such a Good Friday

April 10, 2009, marked the 175th anniversary of the fire at the Lalaurie mansion, and author Carolyn Morrow Long invited me and two other psychics to channel at the home. It was part of Carolyn's research for her biography *Madame Lalaurie: Mistress of the Haunted House*. Though Carolyn is a Smithsonian-trained archival researcher and academic, she insisted that this particular book include psychic elements.

I personally opened the gates at the beginning of the joint channeling session that day. My retrocognition swirled with the desperate confusion of that afternoon so many years before. When that picture was painted in my mind sufficiently, I grounded in them and began to ask a series of questions to those spirits present. I wrote their replies.

During that trance time, I discovered the spirits were all aware they were dead, and only some were still slaves to the horrors they lived in life. Many of them were working on their own dilemmas. Others spirits came to answer the call of that day to share information and to help others.

A strong feeling of the overseer came through me. This was not the male presence, Bastien, with whom I have had contact for decades. This was a ringmaster of all the spirits, an assigned watcher who said, *Laughter rarely rang without witness—her party-face demeanor was quite different than the one that lay behind her mask.*

"Do you fear her?" I asked the spirit.

No—I never did. I am not of this lot. Just an overseer, you may say. Fear is not the right word, for I saw through her.

"Is the darkness still trapped within?" I inquired.

Here and there it may arise, in the midst of passion, anger, and rage. So, no, not always is it visible, but yes, always lurking . . .

During these conversations, a growing stench surrounded us and did not leave until I closed the gates later that night. Everyone smelled it. It was far removed from any "odor of sanctity" ever encountered there before or since. I returned twice more throughout that day and night to check. The smell was still present. I went again on my way home at ten o'clock that night to close the gates. Before I closed the gate tight, I took a series of photos that showed a huge ectoplasmic outline of a woman as well as clusters of orbs and erratic energy streaks. I offered a closing prayer to help those still lingering, then I spiritually closed the gates. I took another picture. This time all was clear. That horrid stench also cleared, and so did I.

Caretaker Tommy Williams related another incident from that evening. Upon request, on that same anniversary night, Tommy was reminded of the importance of this date and was asked to photograph the exterior of the mansion. Those pictures showed the house enveloped in smoke, an ectoplasmic haze. Perhaps astral smoke of yesteryear's fire, for no fog was apparent on this clear April date. Williams was a nonbeliever in the paranormal prior to this job, but he was changing his mind. "Mary, there's just too many things I can't explain inside there. Plus your spirit pictures and now mine, I just can't explain ..."

Countless sightings and experiences are still in report from inside and outside the house, where Madame appears weekly to take her bows to the thousands of visitors gathering near to hear her tale. This feeds her, but perhaps not well enough—sometimes she needs more. Over the years, especially in the year the house was vacant in 2010, I was called in to perform five exorcisms on those who had worked in or visited the haunted mansion; they felt the lash of Madame's phantom whip.

Aftermath and Exorcisms

Karen

Karen called me for help, for herself and her friends, but she was reluctant at first to tell me why. It seems she went inside the Lalaurie mansion just to communicate with Madame and to try out her first attempt helping some of the slave spirits to cross over. Even though Karen's friends were only in the background, looking through other rooms, they were all affected. Guilt by association applied. In the eyes of Madame Lalaurie, and perhaps the collective spirit of the place, they were uninvited, and worse: poachers, coming to take private property or food.

They were easy targets, and their symptoms were typical of an attack. The group's relationships, health, and finances were all deteriorating rapid-fire: Vital energy was zapped; nightmares grew; putrid odors manifested; everyone was fraught with paranoia, fights, and fallings-out with loved ones; and sickness abounded. One of them even ended up in the hospital.

In any psychic or demonic attack, many things and people around you will also get destroyed, leaving the victims vulnerable, weakened, fearful, and isolated. From the inside, it can feel like you are cursed or a bad-luck charm. An attack is an attack: Weaken and isolate, destroy within and without.

I agreed that this was serious. This case has potential heavy dark residual energy, a debaucherous history, and a bloodprint. An immediate exorcism and cleansing to remove the tentacles (attachments) was warranted. Fortunately, Karen and her friends were astute enough to recognize the symptoms of a psychic attack sooner rather than later, so attachments were not as detrimental as they could have been. Think of an attack as a growing infection; the sooner you treat it, the better. Preventative medicine is best: carrying protections and partaking in spiritual cleansing baths and shielding prior to contact. But hindsight is 20/20, so now I had to exorcise. This stage is sometimes called a depossession.

It was a beautiful, sunny afternoon and nearly time for my house call. I woke up feeling ambivalent about the situation and motivation was lacking, but I readied myself to go. The typical impediments began, annoying things. I couldn't find my asson. Where did the special salts that I had concocted just last night go? And the keys; they love to hide my keys. My cell phone was so static ridden that I could not get through to my clients to verify our meeting time. Then the dog peed on the floor. Annoying deterrents for sure, but I was not to be put off.

I gathered my backup Voodoo doctor's kit, grabbed the hidden spare key to the car, and snuck out my own back door, bypassing the blocks. I continued to try to phone the group, but the connection seemed impossible.

I stated clearly "I am going anyway—I am going to fix this!"

I finally arrived at the house. The normally perfect cell phone was still acting up, but I knocked on the door and fortunately everyone was inside. We did a short consultation in the living room: I got each person's separate but similar story, jotted the symptoms down in my journal, and explained the tactics I was going to use. The proprietor of the bed-and-breakfast, Karen, had some concerns:

"This isn't going to remove my house ghosts, is it? I like them," she said.

"No, I am removing the parasitic larvae energies in you, not your house spirits," I replied.

"Good," said Karen, seemingly reassured.

"Undirected banishings can remove everything. I will state my intentions now," I continued.

"I will be performing exorcisms for Karen and her friends. If any of the house spirits present would like to assist and protect us in this endeavor, we invite you to. This is to heal the mistress of this place known as the Dauphine House and her friends. This working is not to affect you. Stay if you can, go if you must."

With Karen now at ease and her spirits notified, we began.

In the kitchen, I cleansed a sacred space and made a circle of salt. I built the altar, anointed candles, and opened the gates with Papa Lebas. I called and fed the loas, my spirit allies, Marie Laveau, Ogun, and Archangel Michael.

During this process, a storm began, and quite a violent one at that. It's always nice when they add a little drama for you. I was amused. But then again, I could also use the power of the storm for my benefit.

An attack will more likely be targeted at a victim's obvious wound or weakness first, even an emotional or astral wound, which they can see—but so can I. I was also cleansed and free of sin to start with, for I knew a little sin-eating was gonna be on the plate.

One by one, I worked things out of them, each having a very different manifestation of the darkness rooted within. When I got to the last patient, I noticed the most grotesque astral attachment of the day. I reached in his base chakra to remove a deeply embedded writhing demon-spawn creature. This ghost lizard–like entity grafted itself firmly, clinging on to the lower spine. A tug-of-war ensued briefly as I grabbed it by its ghost throat. The shadow of its dragonesque forked tail flapping back and forth was punctuated by the strobe of lightning flashes flickering off the marble countertops nearby when—*Bam! Ping!*—the one-inch-thick Pyrex plate where the candle stood shattered and popped with a vengeance throughout the room, ricocheting about as the thunder cracked and the lights flickered. Drama!

"Well, there's your sign. We are done." I washed my hands and closed the way.

I prescribed follow-up treatments to each of them and dispensed protection talismans. I gathered the broken shards of glass, candle debris, and ashes, and bundled them all in the white altar cloth.

My car was just outside the front door. The torrential rain meant I was soaked to the bone in a moment's time. I ran as fast as I could straight to the car, with all the debris items still in hand.

Shit! I should have deposited them in the Dumpster across the street. I contemplated that thought, but I was already drenched and thought I should get the residual debris farther away from the group anyway. I started the car and watched the streets fill with four inches of tsunami-like floods in an instant. I needed to be very careful driving. I wasn't going to give into any fears, but caution was certainly not ill advised. Even for New Orleans, this was an over-the-top rainstorm, and that's saying a lot.

I decided to get rid of the ritual remnants at a crossroads en route, but I shouldn't have taken them with me in the first place. The residuals of what I did could be retained in those items. I drove very carefully, blinded by the rain, praying and talking sternly to dear Madame and company all the way. I could barely see a few inches in front of me. I neared Mid-City at the foot of Canal Street, turning in toward my house, where fifteen cemeteries sit waiting at a crossroads.

Hmm, this way I don't even have to get out of the car, I thought. I could drive through one of the cemeteries in a sort of funeral procession. After all, it is all consecrated ground, and I own property in several of the cemeteries. I have friends and family buried in each and every one, so I have spirit backup, too. I drove in and out of one cemetery, then another, and buried the debris in a nearby Dumpster. Voilà!

Just six more blocks from home, I got rid of the ritual debris, but I still had to do my own personal cleansing ASAP. Though it really didn't seem possible, the rain got even harder and visibility was nil. I was not going to pull over now—just three more blocks to go. Like a blind turtle, I puttered forward, led by sheer instinct alone. I felt my way onto my block and pulled into the space right in front of my house. The second I turned off the engine, visibility was instantly clear; the rain stopped, and the sun shined bright. Ha! I was home.

I opened the car door, and the last thing I remember seeing was the ever-rushing water in the gutter below and my iPhone swan-diving from my lap into the rapids traveling downriver. It was sucked down into the nearby storm drain in two seconds flat. Shit!

There is always a cost. Who knows, maybe my iPhone had residuals too, and it was all for the best. It did cost about two hundred dollars to replace it. I did not charge those clients for any services, but I still paid for helping.

I went to Madame's house the next day to communicate telepathically:

Greetings. Concerning yesterday's events, I do know that those involved were wrong in your eyes, coming in uninvited. But—you cannot harm them. I also know that Karen's attempt at clearing the house spirits into the light might have seemed offensive or annoying to you, but you need to ease up. Her original intention was to just get your side of the story. Plus, Karen works with me. She is pure and will come back here again. Forgive her—she was innocent in intent.

I continued with a bit firmer attitude:

Do not harm her or her friends again. Remember, my family built this house, and you knew them well. I tell both sides of your story out here. You are not allowed to follow or harm Karen, or any of those who live or work in your old home; no harm for myself or any of my guests who visit, either. And, by the way, you owe me a new cell phone!

I looked down as I walked away, and there was an old smashed cell phone a few feet away in the gutter. I smiled. "Nope, not good enough, but funny." I took seeing the phone as a sign but did not take the phone.

Karen was afraid to return to the building. She'd never thought about repercussions from her ghost hunting until this event. I emphasized the importance of standing up to the fear and made her a special gris-gris bag to carry for protection. I convinced Karen that I had calmed Madame down and she would not harm her, and Karen eventually returned to Madame's again. But she is definitely more careful there now.

Karen mistakenly believed, as I may have decades ago, that if your intentions are honorable then nothing can affect you. It's great to be grounded in the light, but it's not so great not knowing what to do when darkness falls. When channeling alone on this situation and with others, I've heard, "Many have tried before to clear this house, many unsuccessfully."

Amanda

Another victim of Lalaurie's charms, Amanda, called for help: "Delphine is following me, and this has been going on for months."

Amanda said she thought her mission was to tell of Madame's innocence. It also appeared that Madame felt some need to protect Amanda. And Amanda did resemble a young Delphine.

Amanda had made two visits to the house. The first seemed innocuous, but she believes this visit prompted her to move to New Orleans. Or, rather, Madame's interest in Amanda is what made Amanda move here. Her original visits had her inexplicably surrounded by ghostly apparitions of the phantom Delphine coming to her bedside. She was intrigued, obsessed.

After that first New Orleans visit, Amanda returned home and her professional and personal life deteriorated rapidly; vicious backstabbing and blackballing occurred. Weakened, but not destroyed, she relocated to New Orleans and hoped for the best.

She was enticed to visit the ghost house on Royal Street again after her move, and it is from this visit that the real trouble began. This second visit to the mansion, she took a hand-pounded nail from the attic as a souvenir and placed it on the windowsill of her new apartment and forgot all about it. It was from that area and a nearby closet that the apparitions and apprehensions stemmed. Night terrors began, along with an overwhelming desire to tell Madame's story. Amanda had the unshakable feeling that Madame was now in her, on her, and all around her.

Then, on several occasions, a swarm of flies slowly congregated in a grouping near the window. No flies were anywhere else—but there were fifty or more in an otherwise impeccably clean and fly-free house. Eventually, she realized this pinpointed to that nail on the ledge.

She decided to look through the pictures taken that day, the day of her last visit to the mansion. There she noticed a shadow, a figure of a woman following her down from the upper floor. Now she was frantic. Messages from Madame were pounding in her head. The flies had been gathering for more than a week. Amanda was becoming hermetic in her own house, and even afraid to go to sleep for fear of what she may encounter next. This was all no coincidence.

She brought me the nail, and I doused it in salt and bound it in an iron box.

Delphine was able to talk to me through her. I knew many of the facts of the case that Amanda did not, so I could test the validity of what she was telling me. Plus, for the record, Madame has an insidious and maniacal laugh—a laugh I have heard on more than one occasion from inside that house, in France, and now through Amanda.

Amanda started by saying that she thought Madame was innocent. There has been a yellow journalism–versus–madwoman controversy for years. When I asked why she thought this, fortunately it turned out not to be the tired yellow journalism excuse at all. But instead of letting the girls opinionate too much, I stopped her and said, "I think it best we do psychic hypnotherapy—a co-channeling session. I will be your facilitator." She agreed, and we began right away. First, I made a sacred circle. Then I gently guided her into trance:

"Take some deep breaths. In . . . and out. In . . . and out. Slowly relax your toes, your legs, your chest, and your arms. Breathe in deeply and release any tension.

"Now we shall slowly leave your body. I will be at your side. You are safe. I will be your spirit's guide. No fears, for I can bring you back at any time.

"Take one step out of your body . . . two steps . . . three . . . With each step, I'll be leading you further and further out of your body."

The descent continued as Amanda easily succumbed further in hypnotic trance. I used a soothing tone of voice, accented with the shake of my asson to hold her energy in a protective cocoon.

"You are safe. I shall be speaking to Madame through you.

"I am inviting Madame Delphine de Macarty Lalaurie. Come and speak with me. Are you there? It's Mary Millan, a Trosclair. You know me as Bloody Mary. Can you hear me?

"Delphine, you have been with this one known as Amanda. I am calling you to speak through her. This is Mary, Bloody Mary. Trust me."

There was a wee bit of fidgeting on Amanda's part and a slight struggle for Delphine to come through.

Ah, yes . . . good family, good family.

"Madame, I am here with Amanda, who says you have something to say to me."

Yes, tell her not to go there, not to go back.

"It seems you're protecting her."

Danger.

"But why, may I ask?"

It's the house. It's not safe.

"She tells me you are innocent, but here there is so much witnessed evidence."

It wasn't my fault. It is the house; the house is evil.

"But Madame, the house itself?"

It lives in the walls, the floors—it's alive.

[Unfortunately I may have met this thing of which she speaks.]

"So, you say the house made you do it?"

Yes . . . I do not even remember all of the things I did.

"But you did do them?"

It seems, but it is as if I were two people.

"I'm sorry you lost your house, your lifestyle. What of Bastien? Did he help?"

He was a good and faithful servant.

"And the doctor, your husband?"

[Cackling, maniacal laughter ensues.]

He was there—some of the time.

"What of Paris?"

[Amanda/Delphine is lost, and a smile comes over her face for the first time.]

Paris . . . the shopping, the clothing.

"I am sure much in Paris was beautiful, but did you long to return to New Orleans?"

I could not; they had taken away who I was.

"Okay, let's return to New Orleans. Not everyone who goes to that house is at risk, are they?"

Perhaps . . . at times, not all the time.

"Would it be helpful to remove something in or under the house to balance it?"

No, it is in the very fiber of the place now.

"Why are you there?"

He keeps us there.

"Who?"

It . . . the house.

"Are there other spirits in the Royal Street house?"

Many.

"Do you interact with them?"

Some of them, but mostly I am alone.

"Should I take what Amanda has brought me from the house?"

Yes, take it. Don't let her have it—keep it safe or it will harm her.

"Am I safe?"

Yes, you know how to keep it at bay. Take it from her and don't let her go back. They saw her—she is in danger.

[Drifting]

With a combination of words, empathy, and strong visualization methods, I spoke to Delphine, reaching inward to find her humanness:

"You were such an incredible hostess, and an impressive businesswoman. You were so strong. The pressure to do what society expected must have felt overwhelming at times. You were widowed twice and stayed strong even when you were left with all that debt when Jean Blanque, your second husband, died. You had your share of romantic troubles with the doctor, too. You balanced it all for a while. Something changed. I am sorry. I wish I could say that romance has changed and extramarital affairs have ceased, but I cannot. The New Orleans you knew has changed; it is changing again now. The Civil War changed many things. The old family names and wealth were heavily affected. You do know slavery is over, right? It was wrong. It was a hard road toward equality for people of color. You lived in the midst of some drastic changing times . . .

"But lets talk about your home. Many owners have been through there, some to your liking, some not. It's important the house be lived in for posterity's sake, even though you may not approve of everyone. It could still be in as bad of a state as the day the townspeople ravaged it and stripped it down to ruins to satisfy their lust for revenge. You could consider helping those who live there. Maybe you could even draw the right match for the house so it could heal. One day, depending on your deeds, you might actually be able to rest, too."

Amanda sat in silence, drifting further and further away, so I brought her back and closed the circle.

After we had done our banishing, after Amanda returned home, only then did all the hundreds of flies in the apartment disappear. There were no carcasses, and no open exits for them to retreat to; they were just gone. Amanda's night terrors were gone after this, too.

Amanda feels better now, and her life is being restored to order. She's moved away from New Orleans, and Madame has not returned. She says she is more balanced now, and though she had a faint desire to return to the Lalaurie house, she says she never ever will. The nail still sits quietly on my protection altar.

Why?

Psychopathy

I find Madame Lalaurie's psychological outlook points best to the narcissistic psychopath. Interestingly, this syndrome is equated with sado-sexual/vampire qualities. It also closely relates to hate crimes.

Roll out the serial killer theory. They look and sound normal, existing within normal society, and are trusted people. They are psychopathic, not insane. Above all, there seems to be no conscience on their part, and any sense of guilt or remorse seems lacking. In many ways, this powerful and rich woman tended to exhibit the dominant characteristics associated more with male serial killers—motivated by passion and implied sexual aspects, plus performing more violent kills versus silent ones.

Females mostly kill those close to them—husbands, family members, and those dependent on them; in this case, slaves—mainly women and children. In this way, Delphine portrays the female serial killer to perfection. Her tortures were more aimed at women and children.

Passion

But was Madame more specific in her passion's rage? Perhaps the aim was directed at suspected female slave lovers and the bastard offspring of her second husband, Jean Blanque. She still owned many as slaves.

Did this fading beauty suspect her present young doctor husband of similar affairs? Did it finally push her over the edge? Perhaps.

Possession

There is one particularly pertinent killer category: the visionary serial killer, those who believe outside forces control their kills. There is no hard evidence to indicate that Madame Lalaurie believed in her possession during her lifetime. It is, however, possible. It has also been verified that she had no idea of the whys of her exile. Many possession cases have no recollection of the acts they committed while in their possessed state. Oral history also claims that Delphine did dabble in the magical arts, which might predispose one to think she at least had some psychic awareness and possible exposure to the phenomenon of possession. Early twentieth-century New Orleanians still claimed that she practiced some form of magic for herself and for others. The specific evidence I have is from the son of a seventy-five-year-old cabbie who, in a 2001 anonymous interview, shared, "There were as many people going to Madame Lalaurie for her magic as there was for Marie Laveau. Dad didn't understand why people don't talk about that anymore. Everyone said that in the late 1930s and '40s."

In my own psychic insight, I did see a more European ceremonial magic around Delphine, not a Voodoo or Hoodoo type. It would be doubtful if she was "for hire," but not unusual for her to have assisted her peers privately.

Whatever alchemy or elixir of life Delphine may or may not have dabbled in, it is safe to say that her magnum opus backfired miserably. Could she have believed she would attain some sort of alchemical eternal youth, or even the ultimate goal of immortality through this work? (In a strange and twisted way, she did.)

Maybe Madame conjured up something that she couldn't handle and was truly possessed by the evil in the house, becoming our bloodlust-filled, hellcat vampyra locked in her own dungeon of flesh.

Soon after the tortures were brought to light, thousands of citizens gathered to realize firsthand the bloodied results of Madame's experiments. Citizens were used to witnessing floggings and public executions at this time, and yet they were still appalled by the horrific showcase of Madame's tortured slaves. Outrage poured onto the Lalaurie property. Since the house itself was attacked by a mob, is it possible that it could have held on to this memory of anger in its residuals and now fights back like a wounded cat? As Madame Lalaurie in spirit form claimed, could it have been the house all along? Was the property inherently evil from the start?

Vanity and Bloodlust

A true trigger points to when Delphine's head snapped back in pain as her young servant girl roughly groomed her hair too bitterly one day. This is when Madame's anger exploded as she wantonly lashed back in vengeance on that wild rooftop chase. Could it be that the passionate pursuit of this waif excited Madame with her first taste of true bloodlust, or was it bred in her to begin with?

This specific tale is eerily reminiscent of an infamous Hungarian countess whom Lalaurie perhaps chose to model herself after. Or maybe authors borrowed from the sanguinary source later in an attempt to make sense of it all. The eyewitness accounts of that sixteenth-century countess, Erzsébet Báthory, relate that when Erzsébet's servant girl groomed her hair too roughly, the countess lashed back and drew the girl's blood. When it splashed on the countess's skin and she cleansed it away, it is said that she realized the skin underneath looked younger and more vital. From that point on, she allegedly drank and bathed in the blood of young peasant girls to maintain her fading beauty. Báthory's tale was printed in 1817, a year after the twice-widowed, thirty-year-old, distraught Delphine had lost her second husband, Jean Blanque, along with her fortune. Certainly a curiosity, if nothing more. We have at least two blood countess cousins in deed; if not in blood, then certainly in patterning.

Blood baths of one kind or another did actually occur within the walls of 1140 Royal Street. Add that "perspiring blood" disease to our own Creole Countess Delphine's makeup as a possible source and reason behind the coveted "skin so fair" of Madame Lalaurie, and we certainly have an interesting reflection in the mirror to ponder.

Some form of blood disease, especially the hemophilia sort, has always been spellbound to alleged vampires of history, along with bloodlust. The human vampire is defined as that which drinks blood for a medical reason, a sexual thrill, or increased psychic awareness. Madame seems to be an all-of-the-abover.

A more logical explanation accuses the young Dr. Lalaurie of performing medical experiments. However, he was not living there at the time, and I am of the lone-woman theory. But perhaps this could also weave into the mix within the mind of our antagonist narcissist, or again maybe it is a combination of these theories—for it is never just one thing that makes us or breaks us. Jealousy, rage, revenge, upbringing, bloodlust, perspiring blood, or even possession can all explain Delphine's blood drives.

Those lacking true power of satisfaction within may lash out at those who are weaker than they are, or succumb to being slaves themselves. Both sides seem to sit within the lascivious Lalaurie. Both master and slave is she—a slave to her desires and her fears, motivated by many reasons, some of which may be buried in St. Louis Cemetery No. 1.

✦

The Spirits' Who's Who

- **Haunted Home/Nest**—This is a rare case where a building itself becomes the entity. Think of it like an attached item with a bloodprint times fifty. In channeling, the overseer said the darkness was "weaved into every fiber" of the actual building. This is rare—this is both a haunted house filled with ghosts and a ghost being the actual house: a ghost of what was, what is, and what is growing. Its job description is observer/participant, and this "smart house" acts as a sort of nest with a hive mentality.

- **Head of House**—The Lady was mostly the true head of house, and her husband Dr. Lalaurie is suspiciously absent from this Royal Street ghostly crew. He and Madame had a separation of "bed and board," and Dr. Lalaurie was not living on the premises at the time of the fire, yet he and the whole town showed up that fateful day. The couple did reunite for a time in France after Madame's escape, but when the money ran out, so did he. Dr. Louis Lalaurie is buried in Cuba. His specialty in life was hunchbacks. Though many took up for his complicity in the dastardly deeds on Royal Street, it was his complacency toward it all that was his guilt. He and Delphine's own children were known to cower in her presence, for she seemed to sup even on their psychic energy.

- **History Keeper**—Servant Bastien has taken the role as history keeper. He is still a faithful servant to the place and its story, but no longer to Madame. I have only encountered him by himself. He even escorted me to the stables down the block with his presence. Bastien now assists the overseer as his trusty servant.

- **Hostess**—A spirit who uses her charming talents to continue to preside at parties in her old home. The light-hearted Lalaurie may appear when parties are in full swing. She feeds on this energy as well, and this might be the best time to help heal her, for her party-planner, genteel-hostess, human self awakes!

- **Larva**—A negative thoughtform that comes to life; a congealed magnetic collective that develops into an autonomous psychic entity. Projected thoughts and memories of people, incidents, and emotions can form into their own life force, (i.e., thoughtforms, egregore). As it grows, it projects its influence. It would be programmed to feed again on what it was made of to survive. It is triggered to awaken when similar energy and emotions are near to reactivate it or when sent or directed from an outside source.

- **Overseer**—This is an assigned watcher over the house. In this particular case, it is not a spirit who lived in the house. This was not the darkness that I tangled with in exorcisms. Instead, this overseer seems to maintain the balance of the area and the people within. It's more of the ringmaster and somewhat positive and tries to protect.

- **Slave**—There are a few slave spirits who are still bound to the situation that their life was embroiled in. These few are stuck. I have tried to console them, but some choose to stay. Delphine's release is intertwined with their healing.

Afterlife Lessons

Always carry protections (at least salt). Never go alone. Be objective; do not judge. Do not provoke spirits unless someone is in danger. (This is exceedingly rare.)

Do not torture or kill people.

Set boundaries; offer consultation, prayer, and patience.

Try to understand each case before following through on any rash decisions, and consider the circumstances of the spirits and humans involved. Use caution, and apply wisdom and a little understanding.

Fear can attract lower-vibrational entities, but so can simply being in the wrong place at the wrong time. The horrors that happen in a place are, at times, blamed on certain incidents that may have occurred there. However, an older theory suggests that there are certain spots in the world that actually draw darkness—areas that crave these low-vibration, blood, and pain energies, and attract them. Look at it like a dark, brooding chakra in the earth's geomagnetic grid. There have always been such places where recurring hardship, sorrow, and bloodshed occur. It is our job to help stop these repetitive issues with the light.

Warnings

The Lalaurie house has been blessed by priests of the Catholic Church on several occasions and by many other denominations of clergy, too. The nuns warned their students on field trips not to so much as glance at the Lalaurie mansion or walk on that side of the block, and to certainly never wander under the galleries—that alone was very dangerous. Some still warn that evil lurks within those walls.

It's wonderful to be balanced and have your heart in the right place, but you can't jump out of a moving vehicle and expect to stay in one piece. Working in the light needs to be balanced with the knowledge of how to bind or transmute the dark—not pretending the dark does not exist.

Disheartening and dumbfounding things will try to block your way if you are on a spirit mission, even one you think is noble. It's all a matter of perspective on who is right, anyway. I try to address both sides and take the spirit's rights into consideration. Even if the spirit is in the wrong, human participation includes manipulating energy that has not only a butterfly effect, but can have a precursor impact on the parties involved, including oneself. Be aware of the risks when you choose to intervene.

In dangerous situations and places such as the Lalaurie mansion, cleansings need to be regularly maintained—once is not enough. Boundaries need to be set and reset. Many triggers can activate an old wound in any house, especially one with such a sordid past and a massive bloodprint. You may need to perform regular maintenance: cleansing, organizing, adding lots of laughter, and saying many prayers to counteract and transform the space within.

You, as the priest(ess)/facilitator, need to be physically strong, balanced, and protected, for removing attachments can be a delicate operation. What you remove can and does transfer into other things. It is best if you purposely direct it to a predestined spot so random attachments do not settle in elsewhere. Make sure you have a vessel nearby dedicated to holding what you remove. I choose only a vessel of water and an iron pot (and maybe inadvertently a cell phone). All items used in ritual need to be cleansed and/or properly disposed of afterward.

Plan, prepare, cleanse, execute, and cleanse again.

Do not be afraid to seek help it you feel attached. It becomes more dangerous the longer you wait.

Listen to the spirits, but never blindly obey. If you are ever told to do something bad to yourself or others, say no loudly and strongly, and cleanse quickly. Never sink into your own shame or depression if darkness is pointed your way. Face it, fix it, and move on. Sometimes your own demons rear up to bite you when you step too close to other kinds.

This particular miasmic haint seemingly spoon-feeding its writhing larvae minions on blood and shame could still feed off of those who wander in unwelcome or unaware. Some serve as sustenance for that which thrives on tasty dark, lowered vibrations. It may have influence. It could be contagious. Make sure you are acclimatized.

Lagniappe

Henriette, the Phantom Who Wanted to Come to America

I HAD JUST COME BACK from a month of sacred sites on a European paranormal family vacation. It was a long, hard, but enlightening summer. We were exhausted and made it home to my cousin and co-priestess Gina greeting us at the door. She had graciously offered to house-sit and take care of our dog Grady and Mamma Kitty whilst we were gone. She had been to my house many times over the years but had never needed to spend the night. She was, however, aware that my house was haunted.

"Oh God, I am so glad to be home!" I exclaimed as soon as we walked in the door. "How did my spirits treat ya?"

"All in all, pretty good," Gina said, "but I ticked someone off one night, and I don't even know what I did."

I dropped all the bags on the floor and plopped on the sofa as everyone else ran to fight for the bathroom, leaving Gina and me alone to catch up. "What happened?"

"Well, I was sitting on the living room sofa watching TV after my tours, like I had done every night. My dog was on my lap, Grady was on one side of me, and Mamma Kitty was on the arm of the sofa next to me. She did the Halloween cat pose and made a horrid *Meeooow, screech.* Grady's back hair hackles, my dog Pumpkin's hair hackles, and a distinct rumbling starts coming from the kitchen. It got louder and louder, and suddenly it turned into powerful crashes and thumps, like huge chunks of plaster falling from the kitchen ceiling to the floor. It rained every day you were gone. I was afraid the ceiling was literally caving in! Then it got louder and faster, but turned metallic in nature. It sounded like someone was throwing silverware all over the kitchen. This went on for more than five minutes. *Well,* I thought, *Matthew's tools are in the attic and now they are crashing through the ceiling and through to the floor to the basement.*

"It finally stopped. My dog's hair flattened down, your dog's hair flattened down. And I found the nerve to enter the kitchen. I was shocked to see that everything was perfect—not a drop of dust or disorder to be seen.

"'Okay, I don't know what I did, but I'm sorry!' I said."

I gave the kitchen a once-over as we entered and noticed a large stack of mail on the stool by the window and a medium-sized box on top postmarked from Europe.

"Gina, when did this happen?" I asked.

"Last Tuesday."

Pointing toward the stool, I asked, "When did that box come?"

"Laaaaaaaaaaaasst Tuesday."

"Hmm . . ."

"Mary, what is in the box?"

The knife was already in my hand. I cut through the tape, unwrapped the bubble wrap, and pulled out a century-old skull, Henriette, and her document: "Fossil de la catacomb Paris, France." In the top right corner was stamped THEATRE DU PARIS.

"Gina, this is Henri. Henri, this is Gina. This is your new home."

Henriette has been quiet ever since.

Since I've acquired the skull, many have felt connections with her and say, "She wants to dance. She wants to dance."

The day I found Henriette in Paris, I had just come from the cemetery, where we were visiting the spirit Madame Lalaurie. I wandered into a little Parisian antique store to ask for directions when this skull diverted my path. I heard a voice over my left shoulder: *I always wanted to go to America.* The need for directions slipped away as I turned and saw a half-hidden human skull.

"Is that skull for sale?" I asked the shopkeeper.

"*Oui, oui,* I have another here," he replied.

"No, is that skull for sale?" I said, pointing. "May I feel her?"

A familiar cold breeze accompanied her transference into my hands. My husband Matthew felt it from afar and turned to meet and greet. I arranged to have her sent ahead by mail so as to not be questioned at every customs border during our travels. Surprisingly, Henriette made it home before we did. Gina was unaware of the purchase.

I think she just wanted out of that box!

My house came with spirits, and I occasionally bring some of my work home with me. I also have a personal collection of empowered and attached items within this haunted home of mine. Some are handed down, gifted, or collected, and these spirits have

Henriette at my haunted house
Photo by Bloody Mary © BMT, Inc.

adjusted to the lifestyle here and become part of the "House," my house. This one requested to come home with me.

I think Henriette may have kicked a mean cancan in her day. Her last gig was in a Paris theater, and she found us whilst we were on way to the Moulin Rouge. She also had her day in la catacombs, where perhaps she met Delphine before she too was shipped back to America.

The Spirits' Who's Who

- **Healer**—Henriette has helped me heal many clients, given a few psychic messages, and healed a client of a shell shock–induced, nonstop headache from the war in Iran.

- **Wise Woman**—Centered on my ancestral altar, Henriette the Elder silently watches with her wisdom emanating through. As oracle, she stands as the heart representing a protective mother ancestral altar spirit. She assists me greatly to protect and heal living children. She was nearly one hundred when she died.

Afterlife Lessons

There is humanness in bones, and they could be seeking out your help. Do a reading or have one done with the spirit who once lived in any bones you may have. Introduce yourself, your home, and your family, and tell them where they are and find out what you can. Ask for their help to smoothe the transition.

✦

Warnings

There are many things we acquire in our lifetime for a reason. Most have passed through other people's hands before we acquire them. To bring an item into the fold in a spirited and protected way, a blessing is advised. If I adopt something of a spirit nature for a haunted collection or an altar, a full rebirthing could be needed. I did a Voodoo couche ritual with Henriette where we drummed and put her to sleep for a week covered in a basket of herbs and re-baptized her upon awakening.

It's important to perform regular cleansings on oneself and on certain artifacts or collections that need to be cleansed prior to aggregating. There is a form of redeeming and rehabilitating within these processes so a spiritual transformation and balance are achieved and adoption is successful. This aids in your home protection as well and is especially important with bones.

4

Jean Lafitte,
the Gentleman Pirate

As I WANDERED TOWARD this old Creole cottage, I couldn't help but admire its restful repose, leaning back ever so gently, as if nodding off in the summer night. Crooked shutters framing its crooked doors supported its bent body of crumbling brick that awakened from its deep slumber as soon as I acknowledged it. I marveled at its mottled plaster facade and distinguished, wavy salt-and-pepper slate shingled rooftop—a bit battle scarred and aged, yet not wounded at all. It just sat there, proudly, like a wise old soul beckoning me near.

A small group of people slowly followed me through, but they became secondary to the world within. For upon crossing the threshold of this old cottage turned tavern, I entered another time. Entranced and caught in its magic web, I let the energy pull me toward the fireplace nestled within and floated toward its center. I slightly bowed as I bent and neared the dual smithy, peering through to the other side, and I became even more out of body and out of time. Waiting within were two floating eyes. Male eyes, no face attached. Just eyes hovering there, staring at me—no, through me! Locked in their gaze, I was under their spell and did not question why no face was attached to those piercing phantom eyes.

For quite some time I held this pose and left my physical body behind. Then the eyes burst into flame. Just like that—*Poof!* Two individual pyres of flame appeared and then disappeared in a snap, breaking me out of the trance. Instantly I was alert, stood up

Lafitte portrait (oil on canvas)
Courtesy of Lafitte's Blacksmith Shop Bar

straight, and shook it off. The beta brain waves kicked into gear, so I crouched back down to search for the mundane source of this encounter, yet nothing at all was there. The sight line through the fireplace chamber was completely clear. I checked. No candles to have blurred, no mirrors to reflect, and no modern fake gas log were there to block the way—just a clear view through to an empty chair and rickety table on the other side. The cold spots continued to cover me in gooseflesh as I explored further within, toasting to the Lafitte brothers, gesturing an old-fashioned salute along my way.

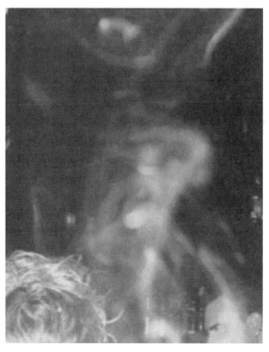

Ghost of Jean Lafitte
Photo by Bloody Mary © BMT, Inc.

A strange familiarity stayed at my side after this encounter for hours on end, and visions of Ole New Orleans flooded through my dreams later that night. I took this encounter as a welcome, and I am still very welcomed by both the living and the dead who reside within this special place now known to all as Lafitte's Blacksmith Shop Bar.

My bloodline memory jar was opened that night. Upon waking, an obsession ran through my veins. I was inflamed and began devouring book after book about Lafitte. That was not enough. I remembered the tales of treasure, swamps, and the dreaded feu follet from when I was young. I went back out to my grandparents' old camp where as a child I listened to the gators croak and was told tales of pirate gold. I traveled far and wide outside the city proper, deeper into the swamps, and asked the oldest people I could find what their grandparents had shared with them.

I am a strong believer in oral history, and those of us who have spent generation after generation here have a different way of expressing these passed-on memories. So I went the extra mile to remember and make sense of it all. Everything told led back to tales of treasure.

The common consensus I heard again and again was that when pirates hide their treasure, they kill someone on the spot, creating a forced ghost guard. This older form of dark arts, generally known as necromancy, could transform the spirit of a dead man or animal into a spirit slave. This ensured that no one could tamper with that treasure except for the person who buried it there in the first place. The problem with those types of spells (besides the murder part) is that there is rarely an expiration date on the duties of said spirit slave. Some of these phantom filibusters are still standing guard at their treasure posts.

Now, of course, Jean Lafitte is long dead, and it is most unlikely that he undid this magic deed before he died. And so it is that this necromancer's spell sentences both Jean Lafitte and the spirit treasure guard to walk the earth bound with a curse of blood unless the treasure is uncovered by someone of noble heart who will put it back into the community for the greater good. So while Jean Lafitte's ghost points the way, the spirit guard continues to block attempts to unearth the treasure. It is said that Jean wearily points the way to those noble few with his long and bony finger and marks the spot with eyes that burst into flame and drip with blood.

Many report that this treasure still lurks in this old fireplace at Lafitte's Blacksmith Shop Bar today. I researched these particulars long after I saw the eyes that guard the fireplace. I was not in search of this that night. I still watch and wait twenty years since this encounter, where this treasure has waited for two hundred years. I do not seek gold for gold's sake, nor do I think gold is the treasure here, but perhaps maps, documents, and clues. But one thing I know for sure is that a treasure trove of history and spirits came in through that fireplace, and that is something I do help unlock. I am a collector not only of objects that hold secrets to our past but also of old memories and histories that beg to be retold in a different light.

The only time anyone has been afraid of the ghost within the walls of this haunted place was when Jason, the bartender, was all alone and attending to his lockup tasks for the night. Suddenly a short, stout, balding man walked out of the chimney and proceeded directly to the end of the bar. This apparition stared Jason down with an evil grimace. Then the figure slowly melted away before his eyes, leaving this bartender incredibly drained of energy and unable to complete his closing duties.

Lafitte's ghost has been reported wailing around many of his bloody treasure spots and has been heard in tales from witnessed encounters as far back as the Civil War. He continues to point the way to treasures, but most humans are too afraid to take these gifts for fear that the curse that comes with it will transfer. According to author J. J. Reneaux:

> A Confederate soldier saw his ghost and heard him moan, "Come with me. I am Jean Lafitte . . . *Viens avec moi*. Come with me! Save my soul! Help me!" The man disappeared . . . [but] the ghostly pirate appeared once more before him . . . "I am condemned," wailed the ghost, "a slave to my treasure, bought with human tears and broken hearts. Now I must pay the price of my fortune. My soul is bound to my blood money. Take my treasure and set me freeeee!"

But what of the gold, silver, and other such wares that fill a treasure chest? Do a few bits of booty still really lie in wait around New Orleans and the surrounding isles? Perhaps some treasure may be found up and down the coast all the way to Galveston, but in Jean Lafitte's memoirs he does confess that a "few caches around New Orleans still lay."

Finding Lafitte in the Battle of New Orleans

In New Orleans, Jean Lafitte is a frequent visitor at Lafitte's Blacksmith Shop Bar where he once lived. His main operation area was an island in Barataria Bay. He called that his commune, but he and his brother, Pierre, had their townhouse in the city to rendezvous, make deals, and cavort. He never owned the building on paper—a comrade known by the alias of "the Castillion" did.

It is said the famous Battle of New Orleans was planned here with later president Andrew Jackson. Lafitte and the men he rallied fought in the War of 1812 with his donated weaponry, ammunition, and skills. Jean offered all of this to the Americans in the infamous deal with Jackson. This battle created the title "Patriot Pirate" for Jean (and his crew) and also helped create a future president in Jackson.

There is still controversy surrounding where the battle was planned. Reports of the ghost of Jean Lafitte stream in from all of the alleged meeting places. It is foolish to try to find the one location of this meeting or Lafitte's presence when one can explore the many.

A plaque in front of the haunted Pierre Maspero's Café also stakes claim to the planning meeting for the Battle of New Orleans. Built in 1788, it was the meeting spot for financiers, filibusters, and freebooters of the day. It was also a coffeehouse and a major slave exchange. The ghost of Jean Lafitte has been spotted in various parts of this important historic building, and he is not alone. The sound of heavy footsteps follows, with icy trails here and there, especially in the entresol, or mezzanine.

Jean Lafitte's Old Absinthe House on Rue Bourbon also lays claim to this meeting, and Lafitte's ghost has been seen and heard here. Jeff, a former employee of the Old Absinthe House, and a pre-Katrina resident in the third-floor apartments above the saloon, saw the ghost. In their book *Louisiana Hauntspitality*, Robert Wlodarski and Anne Wlodarski describe that scene:

> As he was standing in front of the mirror, a bright light flashed in the background . . . a strange looking man was standing behind him, wearing feathered hat, an open shirt, and a red tie around his waist . . . [T]he figure just stared at Jeff . . . the image just faded away.

On another occasion, another employee working the closing shift reports Lafitte's ghost on the stairs near the main dining room area:

> A strange looking man [was] smiling at her. He had very tanned skin, almost leathery; his eyes were brown with an almost mischievous expression and he was between 35–40 years old, with a long curved waxed mustache covering his lip . . . wearing royal blue pants (Napoleonic period), and a fine red shirt with a bandoleer bullet holder draped over the shirt . . . he sauntered over . . . walked right though the bar . . . and just vanished.

All these places and many more have reports of Lafitte's spirit. My answer to all of this is that the battle likely took much planning, in more than one place; and it was probably helped along by much drinking as well!

While there were many meetings to plan the strategy for the Battle of New Orleans, there was only one meeting to strike that initial deal. *The Memoirs of Jean Lafitte* say that he and General Andrew Jackson met on the corner of Royal Street and St. Philip Street, one block from Lafitte's Blacksmith Shop Bar.

The Lafitte–Jackson deal included not only the use of ships, cannons, ammunition, and Jean's superior knowledge of the swamps to aid this victory, it also negotiated for the acts of treason upon these privateers' heads to be expunged. That very same night, Jean's jailed brother, Pierre Lafitte escaped. His jail door in the Cabildo "magically" unlocked, and wrongly-incarcerated Pierre slipped out through Pirate's Alley. This narrow passageway, in between the illustrious Cabildo and St. Louis Cathedral, is now and forever known to have been named after Pierre Lafitte's great escape. This event is reenacted in spirit form still today. I have witnessed the shadow play in Pirate's Alley on quiet nights and have photographed many anomalies there.

The now-named Chalmette Battlefield, where the Battle of New Orleans was fought, has its share of ghosts as well. I met one a cold winter battle anniversary night of 2008 when I offered him the warmth from my HotHands packet. I did not see Jean Lafitte that night, but several other phantom soldiers came forth.

The bicentennial of the Battle of New Orleans victory was a celebration I was sure Lafitte's spirit could not possibly resist. Though his purpose was not to take his bows, as I had presumed, he humbly came through to assist. On January 8, 2015, Gina and I visited Chalmette Battlefield to salute our brilliant war heroes.

The battlefield proved rather barren and icy cold as Gina and I entered and opened the gates spiritually. We strolled through a row of empty tents, watching a few period-dressed reenactors on the sidelines. All and all, on all levels, it was a sad turnout. We managed to burn camphor to cleanse the field and fed it with rum and sweets without being noticed—at least by those in the flesh.

I limped off the battlefield that day and felt both bitterly cold and awkwardly heavy as we exited the grounds to head home. I soon realized I was not alone: A young, swarthy uniformed soldier with a bloody cloth bandage across his head had followed me back. I saw though this spirit's eyes, through his bandaged face, and immediately I felt all of his life's regrets rush though me. Pain shot up and down from my neck to my temple in rapid succession. He was in me. Maybe he *was* me.

I asked the spirit his name, and he said *Albert*. I prayed and began to clear Albert's spirit and then I realized he wasn't alone— he had two fellow comrades with him who were wounded far worse than he. I saw one bent over at the waist with Albert clutching him, holding onto his full weight, while Albert's other arm was around the other soldier's shoulders, supporting him like a limp marionette waiting for the curtain to rise. It seemed obvious that Albert had returned to battlefield to carry his soldier friends to safety; it also seemed obvious that his two soldier friends were already dead. I needed to help all their spirits rise. But first I needed to separate them from my aura. Then I meticulously tended to Albert's still-bleeding wounds. I sent healing vibrations and visuals as I cleansed him, and some of the healing energy transferred to his comrades through him, for all their spirits cleared and continued to get lighter as I explained what was happening.

"I hope you know the war is over, Albert. You can reunite with friends, family, and lost loves. You are welcome to visit anytime.

Let me know if you are not ready to go and we can work longer, but not so close on me, for I am hurting."

I called on the spirit of Jean Lafitte to come give the lads a ride. This was their ticket out. I was surprised that I did this, but I was guided to say, "Your ship awaits!" Jean did the rest. They got on a ghost ship and sailed away.

Once the spirits had gone, I closed the gates and immersed myself in a ritual verbena salt bath. Soon after, neither knee pain nor the heaviness of carrying those soldiers was anywhere near. However, my head hurt for quite some time. I carried much more bloodline responsibility on that field than I took into account, and I'd stirred up some past-life remnants that needed healing. I wonder if Albert was the same spirit I befriended years before when I'd offered a spirit some warmth in the freezing cold. They did look similar, but war-torn soldiers on the battlefield sometimes do.

I returned to the Blacksmith Shop Bar on the most important anniversary of the war to celebrate their victory and toasted the signing of the ceasefire and Jean Lafitte. His humble reply was "You give me too much credit." He was correct, for it is to all those who fought and sacrificed their lives that credit is due. I salute you!

A Wandering Pirate

I am well informed about Jean Lafitte's years in New Orleans, but I have also sought his spirit in far-off places in pursuit of his spirit trail, which is truly muddled. We think he was born around 1780 in either France or French colonial Saint-Domingue. Sources disagree on when and where he died. Regardless of his early and late life facts, he returns here to New Orleans in his phantom form, to

Ghost are present in daylight, but much harder to photograph. Note the rigging
and outline of the ghostship.
Photo by Bloody Mary © BMT, Inc.

the stomping grounds of his glory days. For here he is still a war hero, adventurer, and boss of his own island in Barataria Bay. He reclaims his crown as Pirate King, as he is known to some, and Patriot Pirate to others.

The famous swashbuckler Jean Lafitte does not sit still and still roams throughout his old haunts of life. In fact, "Jean Lafitte's ghost appears so often and in so many places," writes Lyle Saxon in *Gumbo Ya-Ya*, "that it is unlikely he finds time for anything else in the world beyond this one."

In the 1990s, Jean Lafitte was once said to be the most frequent ghostly visitor to nearby Destrehan Plantation. I have even heard that our infamous Myrtles Plantation used to claim Lafitte's ghost haunted the staircase when school-age children toured the property in the 1980s.

In Galveston, Texas, the Laffite Society and paranormal ghost tours report on Lafitte in different ways. There are houses turned taverns there too that his ghost still visits.

Jean Lafitte is also known to appear when summoned. In 1853, he manifested at a séance in Galveston. As recently as August 2014, extended family members in Nashville called on their illustrious ancestor in a séance. Countless other attempts at such contact go unreported.

In Lake Charles, Louisiana, there is an annual festival known as Contraband Days, where Lafitte enthusiasts gather and share tales of pirates, hidden treasure, and ghostly adventures. I have dined at The Pirates' House in Savannah, Georgia, where Jean ventured in life to purchase slaves, and they know his spirit well. Grade-school children in Alton, Illinois, were taught that Jean

Lafitte lived and died there and is buried under his alias name, "Laflin." I traveled to Milton Cemetery in Alton but could find no headstone or spirit sign of his familiar phantom anywhere.

Romance and intrigue inspire us to imagine the spirits of pirates and privateers through rose-colored glasses. Visions of excitement and adventure may blur the hard-life realities that shadow their spirits. I believe in continued growth in the afterlife and in between, and many pirates are still on their adventure. Perhaps some are attached to their treasures as well as their flesh-and-blood existence imprinted in the brick-and-mortar places where they lived and worked, or where their bloodline lingers. Here and all throughout our swamps in Barataria Bay, up and down the Mississippi River, and coast to coast, Jean Lafitte and his cohorts may still roam—especially here in my hometown.

Tales of pirates would not be complete without tales of treasure, and the stories of Lafitte and his cohorts are no exception. They are not alone in their quest, for inside their old home, now the Blacksmith Shop Bar, other spirits flow from behind the bar.

The Cast of Lafitte's Blacksmith Shop Bar

Modern ghosts, colonial ghosts, and everything in between slip in and out of Lafitte's Blacksmith Shop Bar, the oldest bar in the country and one of the three oldest buildings left standing from colonial times in New Orleans. Here, invisible hands grab at your cocktails as you walk by, disembodied voices call you near, and piano keys tinkle a few bars on their own from the rear piano bar. These are just a few of the salutations and encounters waiting within what I have termed the "Ghost Watering Hole."

Spirits play, smoke, drink, flirt, and may even take a few of your personal belongings for a bit just to let you know they are near. (This group of five calls themselves the builders, but don't worry—they will eventually return the loot to you.)

Direct voice phenomena, or DVP, and paranormal photographic evidence are commonplace. Interior video surveillance reveals images that the owner, Detective Joe, cannot explain. At least three phantom men are seen on playback on a regular basis.

I stay late, for when it's quiet sometimes I can connect with the sprits more easily. My Voodoo Paranormal team and I toast and converse with all the seen and unseen around. Nights when we knew we were the only ones left in the place, it sounded like wild parties were going on above the attic office, complete with the sound of heavy trunks being dragged across the floor and laughter seeping down through the ceiling.

Many employees have had encounters, but others have not. This could be because some are just too busy with life's distractions; but also the spirits aren't always present. It is the same with people in our world. We are not always at home. The other side is simply a reflection of our life here on earth.

Veteran bartender Jason and I spend much time conversing and connecting with many of these phantom guests. There are countless past patrons, those who came here in the flesh and have now found their spirit way back for another visit. The spirits sometimes let us know they are listening by rapping loudly on the ceiling. Once, we even did "Shave and a Haircut" on the bar below

Ghost horse in profile bending down to drink water. Note the clear outline of his ear and rigging around his head. In the background, a man dismounting can be seen.
Photo by Bloody Mary © BMT, Inc.

and received a ghostly rapping reply of "Two bits" from the ceiling. Spirits do have a sense of humor and seem to really like this place to kick back and relax, just like humans do.

There is also our petite lady in white, Jeanette, who just may dance with you if you are the one behind the bar. She was once the lover of Jean Lafitte (and perhaps still is). Occasionally, workers are startled by her reflection in the upper office bathroom mirror, and the hidden stairs nearby creak as she walks to and fro. On some nights, she leaves her comfort zone of the upper floor to create an amusing 360-degree spin contra dance with unaware bartenders. They are sometimes accidentally led into a graceful pirouette, ending with a finale of an awkward left-right head jerk as Jeanette disappears.

A very colorful employee and washboard musician, "Smooth," said that when he sees Jean, "He's a man—not a ghost." He sees him in a thick body form, not a misty shape. There are all kinds.

Ghosts pull up on phantom horses and others mingle within the crowd—a pinch on the bottom or a gentle touch could be a ploy to flirt and play. Many spirits are quite funny and jovial. Some spirits could be sad and forlorn, and sometimes they are the same spirits who yesterday were the fun jovial ones who played with you. Moods continue.

Lafitte's Blacksmith Shop Bar has a vortex within, and when it is quiet you might just notice it more as you slip between the worlds and share a shot or dance with these denizens of yesteryear. When it is crowded, there is definitely more happening than just what most of us can see.

Ghosts of Love

Among the varied spirits inside Lafitte's is my favorite ethereal couple, EJ and Rose. This husband-and-wife team of yesteryear is still joined in the afterlife at their favorite bar. If you know how to reach them, they will gladly give you their love blessings from the other side. Offer them a simple gift, a shot of Johnny Walker Black on the rocks.

EJ passed away first, and two or three times each year, Rose and her daughter would made the trip from Texas to New Orleans to share libations with EJ. They had heard about me and my paranormal teachings, knew I was a medium, and wanted to meet me. I had heard about them and wanted to meet them, too. Darryl, a longtime Lafitte's staff member, made introductions one day. I saw the two ladies at their favorite table, one appearing close to eighty and the other in her fifties. I also noticed three drinks on the table.

As I approached, Rose and her daughter invited me to sit.

I declined. "I don't want to sit on him," I said, knowing the empty chair was for EJ.

Rose replied, "Honey, he'll like it."

I took the seat. Then she offered me his drink. I declined. "I'll sit on his lap, but I have my own drink." I figure you should draw the line somewhere.

Rose proceeded to tell me about her husband's deathbed promise: "If you are ever lonely, I will be here waiting for you," he'd said. Rose and her daughter had come to this bar ever since, and Rose confessed that they sometimes planned family reunions in New Orleans so EJ could still be included.

Halloween was EJ's favorite time of year. The old crew would decorate his table with spider webs—his favorite. I offered to continue that spidery promise and asked Rose if she would seek EJ's permission to connect with him. She agreed. They have kept the promise, as I have kept mine.

EJ is a bit of a flirt, but Rose wouldn't change that for the world. He is the one that may untie the back of your dress or knock things out of your hand so you have to bend over—but it's all in good fun. I've had many encounters with EJ and his lovely wife over the years.

One night, after a tour, I was sitting with some friends at a large table at Lafitte's. I had a shot and a cigarette, and I was telling stories about EJ. Soon my friends' eyes drifted to the ashtray in the middle of the table. I followed their gaze, and we all witnessed the cigarette smoking itself: draw, exhale, draw, exhale . . .

So he drinks, flirts, and smokes . . . hmmm.

A few years later, around Halloween, I was at Lafitte's when Darryl ran over to me. "You just missed Rose and her daughter! They were in town."

"Darn, I wanted to share stories and pictures! Oh well, next time," I said.

"No—there won't be a next time. Rose has terminal cancer, and this is her last trip."

I was crushed.

"No, no—she isn't sad," Darryl explained. "She knows they will be reunited and that EJ is waiting for her."

At that moment the air filled with an intense cold spot, like a deep freeze. The guests from my group that night all felt it, and

Ectoplasmic pirate hat on client's head. This was the spirit of EJ coming forth to light up the moment.
Photo by Bloody Mary © BMT, Inc.

one girl complained, "Why . . . *why* is it so cold?!" Everyone put their hands near her to feel it. There's even a photo from that night showing this girl wearing a ghost hat upon her head!

The group dispersed except for two who wanted to connect more. I ordered EJ's favorite shot and changed my attitude. "I toast to a painless passing and happy reunion," I said, and we all clinked glasses.

As we sat, I told my friends my experience with EJ and the cigarette. I pointed to the ashtray with wafting smoke coming from a lit cigarette nearby, and in an off-the-cuff manner I jokingly said, "Okay, EJ, how about a smoke ring?" The most perfect solid smoke ring came from the cigarette, wafted between us, made its way to the fireplace in the center of the room, and disappeared up the chimney.

Rose died about two months later. Not long after her demise, one of her daughters came and spread some of her ashes at Lafitte's to ensure that she and EJ would be reunited there. The family reported that the loving couple has also been seen in their Texas home and at extended family functions around the country.

The Spirits' Who's Who

• **Adventurer**—It seems that Lafitte's lifestyle is imprinted upon his soul, so he simply continues his adventures. But is this just the "unfinished business" blanket reason given to why ghosts roam? In some instances Lafitte is a spirit helping others, but he also has his traveling side—perhaps he is a mere ghost in this persona and these are more of his residual hauntings. But again, you can be both ghost and spirit.

- **Bound Ghost**—Some spirits have been bound and tied to an area by an actual spell or ritual, forcing them to guard or block unwarranted access to prevent displacement of a treasure or gravesite, or other such important tasks. How to break this spell is tied to the releasing of said ghost guard and the prize itself. Releases, reversals, banishings, or calling on a power higher than the necromancer used in the first place could also achieve the desired result. The spell might have included a secret password attached to bypass the guard. Sometimes, a bloodline ancestor of the spell-caster renders passage accessible. In the case of treasure, a sacrificed cock was occasionally added to the mix in hopes that it would do a phantom cock-a-doodle-doo to any ancestor who came near to reveal the way.

- **Comedian**—All kinds of spirit comedians exist as entertainers: musicians, pranksters, all the way to full-blown tricksters. Some will protect you, and some may choose to simply entertain or amuse you. Old New Orleans directories had a very high number of comedians listed as residents.

- **Counselor**—A few spirits are even sent to counsel you or just lend an ear. They sense something in you that resonates with feelings from their own life, so they reach out.

- **Cupid**—This spirit will help others in the area of love. My ghost lovers of EJ and Rose can take this role. This couple is a reflection of heavenly and earthly love, so by that definition

I can say they are Cupids. They do represent true love, family, and fun!

- **Defender**—Jean is a champion of the common man and the underdog. He was a loyal man in life, but he was a smuggler and a slave trader, too. He considered himself a sort of Robin Hood. He may still be on his adventure, but he stops to protect others who are wronged. Jean helps in the area of justice.

- **Empath**—This is usually a human category, but some spirits are empaths too and are sensitive to your needs. Psychic empaths can literally feel the intensity of imbedded situations emotionally and physically. The living empaths may need to take precautions in certain places. In the case of battlefields, empaths won't literally be shot, but they could pick up some of the pain, angst, and adrenaline of the fight. Empaths more often just feel nauseous or ill. Drinking milk before visiting a potentially haunted place with intense residuals can help. There may be stronger protection tools you need to put into motion prior to your trip, and try to be as grounded as possible to avoid getting caught in the line of fire, for occasionally battle might still be going on. Cleanse, purge, and send forgiveness afterward to release stored pain in the area. Bring saltines to help ground you afterward, then eat a meal soon after.

- **Negotiator**—A spirit who can assist in striking a fair deal. If you need help in strategy and negotiations, perhaps ask Jean Lafitte for inspiration and to lend a hand. He had the experience.

- **Past-Life Ghost**—Bumping into your former spirit self is an interesting and sometimes difficult integration process but a necessary and deeper part of soul retrieval. It could cause some disruption as you pull yourself together and/or redeem your bloodline. The battlefield is one example, but I have met other pieces of my scattered soul and had to assimilate, heal, and integrate for my own self and for clients. Bloodline memory could be involved here, for you can carry your ancestors' memories in both their power and their mistakes—there are many ways to relive past lives.

- **Pick-Up**—These are short-term, just-visiting, walk-in spirits who may hover around crowded areas for a one-night stand opportunity. Some bars are pick-up joints for the living and the dead (so is most of Bourbon Street). When an area is super crowded with humans and spirits, they could casually slip into you—enjoy a drink, smoke, or, perhaps, even steal a kiss to feel once again what we in the flesh take for granted. Mostly it is innocent and momentary. Spirits that just want to feel the intoxication can step in much easier when you are inebriated, so drink responsibly. Set boundaries, and remember, just say no if they get too close or won't leave.

- **Prophet**—This kind of spirit will warn you of future peril or guide you to your right path.

- **Rescuer**—A spirit who can assist others when they are wary of their afterlife missions and the roads to get there. Lafitte seemed able to escort a whole crew to their particular spirit ports of call.

- **Residual Imprint Ghost**—Spirits who are the true reenactors! This is when a scene is so heavily etched into time and space that it can become like a movie or hologram replaying itself. Residual hauntings are sometimes explained as echoes from the past, as in past sounds, feelings, or visuals replaying themselves without a sentient spirit actually embedded in them. Residuals can be a trigger for the actual spirits of the reenactors to awaken and slip through the imprint like a portal.

- **Soldier**—A ghost who might still be stuck fighting his or her battle. Some may stay to assist others in their battles or take care of them on the field. Albert longed for love and the simple pleasures in life but stayed to carry his wounded comrades. A good soldier might stay to fight for a cause or to serve as a diplomat. They could be earning their wings by helping you, and you give them a purpose, too.

✦

Afterlife Lessons

You can retrace your steps of life in death. I teach that hauntings aren't just about where someone died; it's really about where they lived—where they grew up, where they went to school, where important decisions were made, where their friends and family are. Everything we do in this world leaves a trail of astral breadcrumbs—the more energy, and the more emotions, the bigger the pile we trail behind and the easier it is to come back.

Have patience: Ghost encounters are not guaranteed. A haunted house is not haunted every minute of the day, nor every month of the year—spirits come and go. Each has its own itinerary and abilities.

Spirits have needs that you can help heal, and they can do the same for you. This world is at least a two-way street (and perhaps more like a busy cloverleaf), and we are usually only noticing one direction at a time. Make a toast, tell a joke, sing a song, say a prayer, share some food. Be one with the spirits, for there can be mutual gain if you allow it to happen. Lighten up and so will they.

Historic events become imbedded in the area they occurred—even more so when they are marked by blood and sweat. Visiting these important historical spots, especially on anniversary dates, can connect you even more deeply with the spirits and history imprinted there. The triggers are itching to fire off on those days, retrocognition flows easily, and the residuals may awaken more literally.

Love can indeed last beyond the grave. According to Emanuel Swedenborg, scholar and father of the Spiritualist movement in 1785, a person's state of mind at the time of his or her death helps create a personal heaven or hell, and "Till death do us part" has no place in reality for happily married couples.

Warnings

Try to clean up your mistakes while you are alive. Gather the pieces of your life to settle in before you die so you do not have to wander; then wandering can be a choice, not a necessity.

PS: Do not curse.

Be careful what type of magic you play with, for your spells and rituals require coin.

NOTE: The fear of curses and finding scapegoats is an easy way out of looking at yourself and taking responsibility. If you believe you are cursed, you may manifest that outcome. Occasionally, curses can be literally sent by others or maybe passed down in a family line, but it is commonly our own actions that cross us up and cause problems. Realize that both your own actions and inactions could create your own curses on yourself. Acts of contrition are advised.

Lagniappe

Blood and Ice

D AZED AND CONFUSED, I stared blankly into a bathroom mirror watching blood dripping down my neck. I didn't know where I was or how I'd gotten there. I simply traced the trail of blood slowly down to my blouse and noticed three females kneeling below me. They were both solid and vaporous and were pawing and pulling at me from the ground. They seemed unable to get a solid hold on me but continued drawing me down toward them. I was in such a nebulous state I could barely fight off their attempts as I just watched more blood trickle out from my left ear down onto the creatures. I was getting weaker and weaker, was stuck, unable to move, when somehow Matthew crashed through the door, kicked the three wraiths off me, and dragged me out. He took most of my weight, and I clung to his shoulder as we walked through an unfamiliar bar.

This astral trip abruptly spiraled and suctioned me back to myself in a flash. My eyelids sprung open in awestruck confusion. I tried to sit up in bed but could not. My out-of-body experience followed me right back to my physical body, and that incident from the astral plane followed me all the way home! This was way more than some nightmare. For now, my own bedroom was literally between the worlds in an even more unfamiliar way.

The air was a congealed invisible gelatin. I barely had the strength to wade through its thickened, ne'er impenetrable mass to simply sit up in my own bed. It felt like my legs weighed a hundred pounds each as I tried to lift them one by one and convince my feet to land on the floor. It was horrendous. Once I was finally up, finding the fortitude to walk through this quicksand matrix was even more challenging. I was the insect trapped inside the aspic that some glutton was surely soon to eat. I had to get out as fast as I could even if it was the slowest slow motion I could have ever conceived.

With great strength and hardship, I found the phone, my purse, and my shoes. Still in my bedclothes, I pushed and pushed, basically swimming through this thickness toward the front door. I knew I had to physically leave or I would die. It was not easy, but any residual fear was replaced by determination. I trudged onward and with difficulty dialed Matthew on my cell, but the connection failed. Now outside the door, I tried again. It rang, but he did not answer. I called again. No answer. I psychically determined where he would be and got into the car and drove straight to the Bank Street Bar. My head was still swimming in that ghostly goop even though I had literally left it behind when I shut the door.

I parked and ran inside and right up to Matthew, and said, "Where were you?"

He was caught off guard. "What?"

I explained.

"Wow. Just twenty minutes ago, I stopped dead in my tracks and worried where you were. I got still for a minute to scan for you. I saw that you were home, so I figured you were safe. I shook it off and continued to play pool."

"Well, thank God you stopped what you were doing to save me. You astrally came and got me out of that hell at the right moment."

I explained more of what happened and ordered a drink. It didn't help.

Later that night, I returned home to a normal house and slept without further incident. But I was still concerned. What the hell had happened? What was it about? Whose crap had I somehow gotten involved with? Was it a client? Had I somehow picked up or angered a ghost? I could not or would not pinpoint it. It was much closer to home than I realized. Even the next day I was praying for the meaning of the previous night's experiences, for it was one of the most surreal and horrific things I had ever encountered.

I called Jagger's dad for help. "Chris, please keep Jagger tonight. I had no real sleep last night, and something's just not right." Chris wasn't really a believer in supernatural events, but when he asked what happened, I told him.

"What time was this?" he asked.

" Eleven pm-ish," I replied.

In an off-the-cuff and rather strange matter-of-fact way, he said, "Oh, that's exactly when I was sitting on the toilet with a gun to my head and my wife was trying to stop me from killing myself."

"What!!! What the hell? Kill yourself?"

Then I realized what had happened.

"Then I took that bullet for you, Chris. I was bleeding and really almost died in that bleak alternate world of yours you sucked me into. I could feel it all. Plus, what were you thinking? Suicide? That is not an escape or an end to the pain you are feeling. After death, you still have to face the same things, just in an unfamiliar place in the spirit world. Then you might be born again just to have to do it all over again until you get it right. It will be worse the next time around, compounded with all the penance or karma required from this dumb choice, which would be a horrible mistake! Please, Chris, there is worth in your life even if you can't see it now. You can survive this. And what about Jagger?"

I tried everything. Now I was on edge, because he was on the edge. I had to protect my child, our child, from his dark thoughts. I had to try to help Chris find a reason to live.

I thought Jagger, whom Chris loved, would be enough reason to live. I really hoped and prayed that it would be. I was out of sorts and worried. No longer was I concerned about the meaning of the previous night's experience. It was obvious. I was amazed that I was still so connected to Chris that I actually stepped in to take that bullet. I then realized that I was in his bathroom in that vision, and that it was his life on the line.

My work went to the side. I went to Queen Marie Laveau for help. I went to my mom, who had sensed something was wrong weeks before. I'd ignored her concerns at that time—after all,

Chris and I had not been together for eight years. I was too blind or had blocked his personal marital drama out of my life long ago, or so I thought.

I asked Chris to meet me at Lafitte's with the intention of getting him to sit by EJ and Rose for a love boost. He was the only one who ever refused to sit down with them. He listened to their tale and said he too wanted a love that lasted beyond the grave, but he wouldn't sit. Chris's wife had cheated on him, and he was not able to handle it. I tried to do a cleansing and a banishing to shake this growing darkness off of him, but Chris would not let me totally in. It was a grueling and devastating job, and the *only* suicide that I have tried to stop and failed at. It was horrendous.

Many other horrific paranormal incidents occurred with that dark suicide demon on Chris trying to get at us. There is an actual entity with a form of possession on the weak and vulnerable when they are in this state of confusion leading to suicide. I saw it, I fought it, with great cost to myself and my family. It did not get fully into us, but it tried. In the end, it won.

The funeral was held at Shoen's in Mid-City. It was hard. Jagger had not seen his dad in the week before his death. I was afraid to go to the coffin with Jagger, but I tried to be strong. I asked Jagger if he wanted to view his dad, and told him he did not have to, but I knew that closure would be important later. He wanted to.

We walked solemnly up to the coffin. I watched Jagger's face as he looked at his dad. I was bracing for a breakdown, but it didn't occur. Later, Jagger told me he didn't believe his dad was truly dead until he saw him in the coffin. I had seen Chris in that exact style coffin weeks before—a 3-D psychic vision while I was fully awake that I wish I had not been privy to.

We were going to get a lock of his dad's hair. I had the scissors open and ready in my hand. I clipped a ringlet. With hair in hand, I turned to my son and said, "Your dad has a Christmas present for you."

"How?"

"You will have your first white Christmas."

I heard the words and was in disbelief. I wanted to kick myself and cry at the same time, but I did not let on that I was upset. Why would I promise such an outlandish thing to my son at the moment he saw his deceased father? This is New Orleans. We did not get snow. *Arrrrrrrrrrrr!* This was one promise that his father better keep.

Chris's spirit sat on the organ in the chapel room, dangling his feet during the service in a nonchalant way for a bit. I was distraught on many levels, but especially since I'd said something I feared I might regret.

Everyone followed us in the limo to Greenwood Cemetery for the burial, and then we went for a repast at my house. Nadine, Johnny B.'s mom, helped set up the food. She was such a godsend, God rest her soul. Johnny B. was Jagger's best friend, and thank goodness he was there for Jagger. A few of Chris's friends were there, and Chris's parents had flown down from New York.

I realized I needed to get some of Chris's prayer cards from the car to distribute to the guests. My car was parked right outside. I went alone, only to discover that the driver's-side window had been shot out. That shattered my wall of composure. I cried. I screamed. "Chris, you didn't have to do this!"

I was not only talking about my window. I went back upstairs and tried to keep my composure. Chris had killed himself in his car. The bullet had entered his right temple and exited through his left ear, shattering the driver's-side window. Some people understood the significance of this event, and some said it was just a coincidence. I do not really believe in coincidences, and I do not live in a neighborhood where windows are commonly shot out. Little did I know that more shot-out window supernatural scenarios involving Chris's spirit bullets were yet to come.

The weeks went on. Thanksgiving came and Matthew was very sick. The month leading up to Chris's death, with multiple suicide attempts and trauma, had been very hard on all of us but seemed to affect Matthew physically. It was almost as if my mystical maneuvers to try to keep Chris in this world were causing Matthew to lose his life force. Matthew was septic, in bed, and I had been nursing him on top of juggling the demon of suicide off Chris while protecting Jagger. Matthew got better just in time to be a pallbearer for Chris's funeral and then relapsed again. The stress of it all was getting to be too much for all of us.

A very warm Thanksgiving went by, and now all that was on my mind was Christmas.

It needed to snow. He promised it would snow. It had to snow. This channeled promise was on November 6, when it was still pretty warm outside. Christmas in New Orleans could be bloody hot or bitter cold, but snow was not the norm. The last thing I wanted was to break Chris's last promise (my promise?). Christmas Day neared, and it was a little colder, but just barely, and no snow was in any forecast.

I woke up early Christmas morning and the skies were clear. We drove to visit Chris's grave and give him some Christmas cake on the way to my brother's house for dinner. As we turned into the cemetery, slush began to fall. I was elated and told Jagger that it was snow—he had never seen snow. The second we got out of the car at the graveyard, perfect white snowflakes began to fall, and they kept coming. It wasn't just flurries—it was real snow! We made snowballs and tried to throw them to the top tier of the mausoleum vault where Chris was laid to rest. It was actually a white Christmas. We all danced in the graveyard. All of us were literally dancing with the dead. I cried and laughed at the same time. It was the first time we had laughed in a very long time.

It was a supernatural Christmas miracle. We made mini snowmen and kept them in the freezer for a long, long time. It was a happy day.

Five months after Chris's death, I miscarried. It happened on April 11—Chris's birthday. Nine months after that, Hurricane Katrina came. Chris was there with us for both of those events.

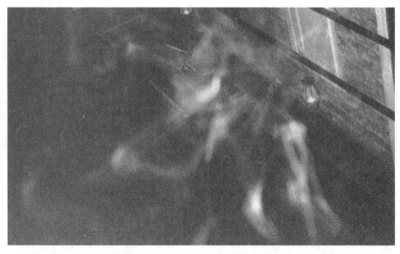

Angel spirit blowing a trumpet with arms bent and a hat upon his head
Photo by Bloody Mary © BMT, Inc.

Now, ten years later, Chris's spirit is somewhat released, partially because his son grew up well and became a happy, good young man. I have spirit visits from Chris, I stayed as counselor for him to help him through his trials in his journey on the other side. Chris had to let go of the fears possessing him, which took over his spirit in his end days. In mediumship sessions, it seems that Chris is now in his study phase—going over his life decisions one by one.

The Spirits' Who's Who

- **Spirit Father**—These are fathers on the other side who still watch over their families. Chris comes to watch his son grow. They have not been able to truly interact, but he protects us. Jagger has put up his own blocks on this interaction. Chris still makes time to pop in and watch over us. He did so during Hurricane Katrina, and he was at his son's high school graduation. I felt him deeply at Jagger's recent college graduation, too.

- **Suicide Preventionist**—Spirits who choose to help others who are in a similar suicide state as their own end days. I solicit Chris to help me when clients are on the brink of suicide. I ask his spirit to intervene. He is good in this job that he has chosen to accept to assist others in need.

Afterlife Lessons

Blood is thicker than ice. Divorce on the physical plane does not erase the connection you chose in life, especially when a child is created with that liaison. There is a responsibility and love that links you forever.

I have learned patience—after all, time is on our side, not theirs. I did not interfere with God's natural plan in death's journey but held Chris's hand, so to speak, and helped him with his hurdles. I understood there was work he needed to do.

Rites of passage are common spirit visitation times, as are holidays.

Warnings

Suicide is not the end. It is not the answer. It is not an escape. We cannot evade life's learning lessons and must face them, or they will continue. If you are lucky, you will have someone over here and over there to help you heal. (Mercy suicides are usually different.)

The people you hurt by killing yourself are your karmic responsibility, for you are not just killing yourself when you pull the proverbial or actual trigger of death.

Inner demons can manifest from the unconscious and bite you, but other demons can, too. There are demons of various types and strengths—demons of disease, drug addiction, suicide, lust, etc., who wreak havoc. I have wrestled a few for patients, including this particular suicide entity. The host must want it to leave, be strong, and not give in to their fears or shame. The facilitator must also be clear and grounded.

Forced crossovers could be meddling and create a form of culture shock for the new spirit, perhaps causing a premature return if not handled slowly, step by step. It is similar to doing a quick fix to mask symptoms of a sickness and not taking time to get to the root of the issue. Address the soul's healing needs at the core.

Dying in a quick, confused, and anguished state, like most suicides, can detour proper passage after death. In Chris's case, he tried a quick rebirth approach on his own, but it did not set because it was not the right time or place. I remain Chris's death midwife, and his widow, but I was not supposed to become his mother.

5

Cities of the Dead

The Shadow of Death

*The dead are not forgotten in New Orleans . . . Other places
in America have made death an antiseptic phenomenon. But
among New Orleans families tombs have primitive power.*
—RANDOLPH DELEHANTY

ONE DAY, WHILE QUICKLY rounding the bend of a mausoleum, I was taken aback by the smell of rank, rotting flesh. It was fresh, strong, and extremely nauseating.

"Oh my God! Something must've just died, and it must be the size of a cow."

I pulled my turtleneck over my nose to block the smell as I gagged and wretched and began to search the area for a carcass. I looked up, down, and in between. Something this dramatic could not emanate from a small creature. Why can't I find the source? This is not a smell that's normal in a cemetery. Not these days. Maybe in our plague times, but not now. I kept searching and would not have been surprised if I had found a heap of rotting animals piled eight feet high. It was that intense.

I was still holding my breath, but I had to breathe sometime. I took the chance and dared a shallow breath. Hmm. I took another. I slowly lowered my turtleneck and breathed deeper. The smell was gone. I realized this smell had come from the other side. It was then that I saw a shadow figure at least eight feet tall, rather bulky, and very wide sneak between two tombs nearby.

"Hello," I said. "I get it—you are big and scary and smell bad. That's okay. I am not scared, but I'll leave you be."

This was the first time I saw that shadow man, but it would not be the last. He always seems to be lurking in the sidelines at the same spot, off and on for many years, though he only emitted that smell the first time we met. We had a mutual understanding. I greeted him and respected his privacy, and he in turn respected my nostrils.

I did realize that this same smell was a familiar one in New Orleans in times of great disease and plague of yellow fever. Piles of corpses and death trenches filling the streets were a common summer sight in the nineteenth century when we had the highest mortality rate in North America. Three out of four people were wearing mourning black at all times, and the streets were littered with *vomito negro*—the dreaded black vomit. This was the last stage of yellow fever before death when you regurgitated your own undigested blood, which had the consistency of wet coffee grounds, black as night. It also had the smell of a fresh rotting corpse, an old and very familiar scent throughout town. They say it is a smell you will never forget. I won't, and obviously my shadow friend did not, either.

A few years after I'd first spotted the shadow, I had a very unusual and annoying experience in the same graveyard. I was waiting for a small private class and they were very late. When they got there, there were only three people instead of five, and then one of them wouldn't get out of the cab. This hesitant one wasn't necessarily afraid of ghosts, but she had never been in a cemetery before. She was concerned about disrespecting the people buried there. I explained that I did a lot of cemetery restoration and a lot of work with the spirits within to help them clear their path, and the woman readjusted her fears and exited the cab. In fact, she ended up being the normal one out of the group; the other two friends were out to lunch.

They all claimed they were psychic and understood the spirit world, but that was not the case. We took barely three steps inside the gate and two of them echoed each other with bloodcurdling shrieks. Absolutely nothing frightening was afoot—except perhaps stepping on a few dry, crunchy leaves. I was jolted by their childish behavior and told them to calm down and continued my way in. We walked a few more feet while I told them some of the history of the place, and again I jumped as their ridiculous, piercing screams hit my ears. I recovered, and then another leaf, another scream. I insisted they needed to stop screaming or we would not continue. They promised to behave, so I grounded them once more and proceeded.

We continued walking with various gasps and giggles at any bug crawling by or rustle of wind. Somehow I managed to greet the spirits properly. I tried to explain how our cemeteries and spirits work when I could get a word in edgewise. I also tried to explain that reality is not like a Hollywood movie to enlighten and hopefully calm them down:

"Ghosts aren't going to reach up out from their graves and pull you in and try to hurt you. They are not stuck in there; there is an attachment to their bones, where they are buried, where they are memorialized and visited, but their spirit is not stuck in the coffin with the remains. Some might step back here on this side if there is a familiar face, a kindred spirit, or even just a funny hat. There are a million reasons to trigger their visits.

"Spirit connections can occur for funny reasons or deep, meaningful ones, like when they recognize you as a bloodline connection. Some may need your help, and when that happens I try to provide it to them. Other spirits may not even be buried in the cemetery they haunt—they could be spirits of visitors, workers, or mourners. But it's not going to be grabbing at your ankle, pulling you in or jumping out, and going 'Boo!' So relax."

I am not sure if these two women were actually listening to me or not, but if they didn't listen to me, I hoped that maybe the spirits would be able to get through to them.

We continued ahead, and I rounded a corner into a whole different cemetery. The girl at my side was the quiet one who would not get out of the cab at first, and the two others were clinging onto each other about ten feet behind us. We continued talking and walking quietly, and then I heard odd noises behind me. I turned to see the two girly girls bent over, dry heaving, gagging, and making dramatic, disgusting noises. I quickly turned to my side companion and said, "Oh, it figures, they're drunk!"

"No, no, they're not drunk," she said. "I've been with them for three days. We don't drink—we never had a drop."

Screaming like little fools, and in the midst of dry heaves and drama, one of the others manages to speak: "We're not drunk. It's that smell!"

I walked closer. "There's no smell." I turn to the woman at my side, and she shrugs. She doesn't smell anything, either. "We don't smell anything," she says.

"*What?* Something must have just died. It smells strong and big. We should go look for it!"

I started to argue and then realized that we were in the same spot where I was a few years before.

"No, I don't have to look. I've done that before," I explained. "There is nothing here—nothing physical, at least."

"What? You don't smell that?" (Gag, gurgle, retch.)

"Nope, it will go away in a minute. Just wait."

I then saw my shadow friend slip between the tombs and pointed him out to the quiet one.

"How can something like this just go away?" one inquired in between gags.

"Don't worry, trust me."

As I predicted, within thirty seconds the smell had disappeared.

I winked at the shadow guy as we walked away in blissful silence. The incident seem to humble the screaming hyenas, and I hoped our problems had been solved as we continued on our journey. Then, out of nowhere, there was another attack of a dreaded crumbled leaf. I rolled my eyes in response, but this time their screams rolled them right back into bent bodies, dry heaving and gagging, over and over again. I smiled, knowing that the nauseating smell excluded me and the woman at my side, and was comforted in the fact that even the shadow man had grown tired of their screaming and done something to shut them up. Not only am I not afraid of shadow people, but I will also work *with* them. In fact, I always knew this particular one had my back if anybody or anything tried to mess with my guests or me. I have walked everywhere without incident and have allies in many places—even in the shadows.

Burial Process—The Inside Story

New Orleans in and of itself is a city of the dead. Then, of course, there are our cemeteries, which in and of themselves are anomalies to outsiders, but not to those of us who are native born. Locals have spent a good part of their childhood within the Cities of the Dead. From a microcosmic or macrocosmic perspective in New Orleans, anomalies are usual, and paranormal is the norm.

Most of us have encountered the unusual and the unexplained in our visits to cemeteries. We are not that surprised if live music is playing for the dead, if a bone is lying in our path, or if we see an old, broken-down coffin in a Dumpster. Nor are we shocked if we discover offerings of cooked food, liquor, toys, or even the occasional Voodoo ritual remnants—it simply is.

Citizens still jog and walk their dogs through graveyards, and many of us even learned to drive in our larger cemeteries, which have street names, stop signs, and meandering roads. It is to the stranger in our midst that these things seem odd. Even our

Greek revival three-shelf family tomb of the Widow Paris in St. Louis cemetery no. 1. This is the most-visited tomb in the country and the sacred shrine of Voodoo Queen Marie Laveau.
Photo by Bloody Mary © BMT, Inc

aboveground burial, reuse of family tombs, and jazz funerals with blaring brass entourages followed by dancing with the dead seem foreign to outsiders.

Much of this is the norm in Latin Catholic areas, but some traditions are uniquely New Orleans. Unfortunately, many of these things could be forgotten by future generations in post-Katrina New Orleans, with over half our residents being recent transplants without the benefit of generations of family upbringing that we, the Creoles, had. Up until now, March 2015, New Orleans did not dictate how to mourn or acknowledge *le morte*. We retained a little of our je ne sais quoi. But now, our oldest, and one of the most fragile, cemeteries, St. Louis Cemetery No. 1, just closed to non-escorted tourists and non-property-owning residents. There are also new restrictions on gifting the dead within: Food, candles, beans, and pennies are all banned. It seems even flowers might not be allowed. Much to my chagrin, and with tearful eye, I witness firsthand and report this part of our culture dying. Though these restrictions are allegedly for protection and preservation, rights are being removed and cultural traditions are being buried in the process. The "antiseptic" is beginning to be applied. The spirits are not happy about the changes, and there is a great division of opinion in the living citizens about it all as well.

New Orleans does indeed do belowground burial—always has, always will. It is quite misinformed to say that we cannot. In fact, New Orleans only did belowground burials until around 1789. Then the aboveground family tomb style began to build its skyline. Plus, aboveground burial was the perfect way: With a shortage of dry land in this giant swamp, coupled with an extremely high mortality rate, the aboveground burial style and accompanying reuse angle allowed maximum potential to be realized. The practicality and beauty of aboveground burial became part of New Orleans's landscape, but many other factors contributed to us sharing eternity with our kindred dust inside these aboveground sarcophagi.

New Orleans's high water table is not why we boast magnificent cemetery architecture; the Greek, Roman, and Egyptian architectures that were in style in Europe during the late eighteenth century became embedded in New Orleans during Spanish rule. Aboveground burial is employed in all Latin Catholic areas—Central America, South America, France, parts of Germany, and many other places around the world—just generally

Yes, there are below-ground burials. This is a freshly dug grave
guarded by a not-so-fresh face on the side.
Photo by Matthew Pouliot © BMT, Inc.

not North America. (Remember, we were not always American!) It is a European style for our displaced European city.

Most of these brilliant and incredibly gorgeous architectural designs become inheritance as they are passed down to family members. Tombs become part of probate and are essentially considered property. They can be mortgaged, sold, and occasionally are even threatened with eviction. They also increase in value as time goes by. Most families will use a tomb for generations to come, and because of this our cemeteries are never truly filled. We were "green" early on. Even in our belowground sections, almost every cemetery plot in New Orleans is reused—with the near exception of the Jewish graveyards.

The process is thus: When the previous family member's body has totally decomposed, another family member can reuse the shelf or plot that the previous coffin was resting in. The first coffin is disposed of, and the human remains are generally placed in the tomb's *caveau* ("cave"), a contained basement two to five feet below the tomb. This leaves room for another family member to use the gravesite while the previous remains literally do join their kindred dust. The weight of the new incoming bones aids in the natural decomposition process in this caveau—ashes to ashes, dust to dust are somewhat achieved in this ossuary. This enables each niche or vault to be reusable for many future generations. But not all aboveground burial tombs have a caveau. So in these cases the old bones are placed in the dead air space around the coffin, or maybe even inside the new arrival's casket.

To reuse belowground burial plots, the old coffin is dug up, the physical remains of the previous tenant are removed and placed back in the earth, and the old coffins are disposed of. Then the new coffin containing the recently deceased family member is placed in the hole on top of the old bones. The law is to dig down at least four feet. Later, that displaced earth is used to create at least a two-foot mound atop the new arrival. The rain and such pushes the mound with the coffin farther down into the earth over time and leaves a rather secure groundcover.

It is important to keep at least two feet of earth on top because some of the earth can easily be washed away by excessive wind, rain, or tidal surges (this last situation is rare). But not all adhere to that rule, and occasionally a coffin is exposed from the get-go. With just a few inches of earth hastily shoveled on top, this may give the illusion of coffins "rising" when in fact these were never buried properly to begin with. There were rumors that during Hurricane Katrina coffins rose up and were floating all around town. That really did not happen in the Orleans Parish cemeteries. Alas, it is the process—not the water table—that is to blame, if and when this actually does occur. If the belowground burial process is done correctly and monitored, this is not usually an issue.

However, sometimes the displaced earth mounted on top of a new arrival does contain concealed bones of previous family members within our clay-clumped earth. They can work their way out to say hello with time and rain. Bones can be seen mixed with shell and soil in almost every single cemetery in New Orleans. I have personally reburied hundreds.

Many have heard that after a year and a day the remains get the shaft. But with modern embalming techniques, decomposition can take seven to ten years or more. It is not an exact science. However, long ago it was indeed a year and a day before reuse. The year-and-a-day rule was our custom, not a law. By that point, the body was thought to be past the point of spreading disease (always a concern). A year and a day was believed to give the soul time for its full journey. And by then, the body would have been totally decomposed. There can be no flesh, muscle, or other tissue clinging to the bone for the ossuary to work correctly—it must be dry bone.

The forgotten and most important reason to wait a year and a day before moving the remains is that this was a proper ceremonial time used by many religions as an initiatory period, because a year plus one day would have been a completion of the lunar and solar cycles. There was no official "un-burial" at the end of the year and a day, unless there was a deceased family member waiting in line for the spot. It could be more than a year and a day, but it did need to be at *least* a year and a day.

People worry if this practice is disruptive to the spirit within. Does it anger them? This is doubtful, since it is a custom carried out around the world and is done with reverence and respect for the people and spirits involved. It is mainly Americans who have this fear that this is disruptive. But certainly to destroy or dishevel bones with ill intent would be a different story.

Though each spirit has a personal journey to follow after their physical death, there is still a memory in the bones. Scientifically, you can say it is in the DNA or genetic memory. There can be an attachment to the remains, and this memorial space is strengthened by visits from family and friends. These are just a few reasons why graveyards may have spirits connected. A person's spirit is *not* stuck in the coffin with the remains, but you might say that a memory is.

Occasionally, spirits may visit their cemeteries, as well as the places where they once lived, and they are able to connect with and protect their extended family. They are here, but not here. They can come and go, as desired, required, remembered, and prayed for. Some are more mobile and communicative than others. The reasons for this are as individual as one's unique personality traits and spiritual awareness. Each spirit's progress after death is unique.

I have met myriad spirit personalities that step through the veil all over town and in every single cemetery. Each cemetery also has its own guardians or caretakers from the spirit realm. Some cemetery spirits are these watchers, some are new arrivals, and others may be spirits of employees and visitors just stopping by. Spirits may pop in to share messages or to request simple things to fulfill a need. I have hundreds of such cases.

Grave Encounters

And then there are the children. The particular cases below were all from different New Orleans cemeteries.

Emily

A little girl in a plain brown cotton smock dress with long straight brown hair sits silently on the step of a coping tomb. This is Emily, and she is seen quite often, generally still and solemn. Occasionally, she is in the nearby bushes and will rattle the branches to signal her desire to communicate. I've brought her a few toys in the past. She is in want of a mother. Some have felt her hold their hand, and some have seen her more vividly. I have, too.

Not all receive the message in the same way. Sometimes this is by choice; the spirit wants to direct their message to a specific person or just a few. Sometimes, it's all in the eye of the beholder. In one encounter, a woman saw her in a thick, distinct human form, while at the same time I saw her in a totally opposite way. The other six people in our group saw nothing, but some felt different, had cold spots, or were moved to tears for no apparent reason as they were pulled into the stream of the encounter.

Emily carries a little rag doll. She wanted a stroller for her doll, so I got her a small one. The message from my student, a schoolteacher, was Emily desired a specific type of baby carriage—old in style, with large, round rubber and metal wheels and a canopy. Over the years, Emily would reach out to the mothers of young girls and schoolteachers of children near her age. She was specific and selective about whom she chose to appear to and when, and I always questioned those who came upon her. I never mentioned anything about Emily until someone else brought up an encounter. I didn't want to lead anyone into a projection. Spirits can read you and your life. The women to whom Emily appears have these things in common.

This dramatic incident sent a schoolteacher pacing in reverse, repeating, "Oh my God." A step backward.

"Oh my God." Another step.

"Oh my God." Yet another step.

"What are you seeing?" I asked.

She described Emily perfectly. "A plainly dressed young girl around the age of seven or so years old, wearing a brown cotton smock with lighter brown straight hair. It's partially pulled back in a barrette away from her face and loosely hangs down below her shoulders. She's holding a small baby doll."

"Can't you see her?" she emotionally questioned me. "Can't any of you see her?"

I replied, "No, not this time, but I have seen her and felt her many, many times before. I can tell you exactly where she is."

I walked to the spot. My visual was intensely different from hers. Instead of seeing Emily's tiny figure, I saw bright, blinking orbs creating an arc of energy shielding, materializing, and feeding her manifestation. I walked directly to the center of this paranormal event, enveloping Emily in a huge astral hug.

The woman screamed, "You are right on her. In her! Stop!"

"It's all right," I explained. "I am connecting with her."

I let the energetic waves and tingling chills run right through me and sent a mother's love as strong as I could to Emily. I had no fear of walking to and through her spirit. The woman was perplexed that I could not see her the same way as she did and wondered how I knew where to go. I tried to explain.

"Well, I saw an arc of orbs—distinctly visible, very bright with rods and a halo glow around her aura and shape of Emily, very angelic. Orbs can come alone, before, during, and after a manifestation, and are more than one thing. But this was intensely electric and moving."

The existence of orbs and their significance are subjects of great debate. But I can see them with my physical eyes. Some believe orbs are just the raw state of a ghost; but I also see them as an energy source, and I believe at other times that they are holes between dimensions—portals. They also vary greatly in size, strength, and color. The stronger the manifestation, the faster and brighter they seem to pulse. I have also communicated with one orb pulse for yes and two pulses for no in a type of visual signal Q&A response system.

This particular encounter was the brightest and most intense orb cluster I have ever seen. I realized they always pulse, sometimes quickly, and sometimes so slowly it looks as if they disappear and/or move to another side and then reappear. At first I thought they were jumping back and forth, not realizing there were many of them pulsing in and out in their supernatural light show. So, in this case, it finally became clear that it was not just one moving back and forth, but many, many more that were forming, surrounding, and even becoming the spirit.

"Emily knows how hard I try to explain these things to people, so she revealed to me only what I needed to see and let you see what you needed to see," I explained.

Interestingly, I did not see Emily's spirit apparition in this encounter, only her energy source—and this source was alive! I could see how some may misconstrue this visual as being extraterrestrial in nature.

Emily just wanted love and was sad without her mother. We provided some of the comfort she missed. She also provided knowledge from the other side. There were other spirits around her that I had encounters with, but Emily didn't seem to be able to interact with them. I try to connect spirits together. Sometimes it is possible, but other times it is not.

Emily always showed up alone with her little doll friend. Perhaps she only wanted to seek a little of the human love that she missed, through myself and the many mothers and teachers that

I brought near her so she could remember, or maybe so she could be born again.

Our love helped release her spirit, and Emily seems to be gone now. My crossing over into that arc sent a very direct love emotive healing energy to her. I still visit her old haunts to check up on her just in case, and I sit and send prayers and sing songs.

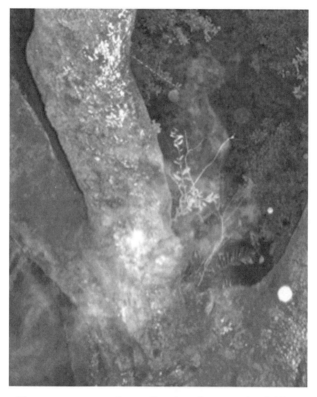

There are many ectoplasmic faces here, but note the child up in the foliage of the tree staring into the camera. The head is slightly above and between the two orbs.
Photo by Bloody Mary © BMT, Inc.

Richard

Richard seems perhaps nine years of age when he shows himself. He was a difficult one to figure out at first. There was an area around him that had a somewhat foreboding or "stay away" energy, and I can guarantee you that most people would have interpreted that as evil. Richard was not evil. I respected the KEEP OUT phantom sign that was posted and walked around that area out of respect. His tomb, hidden under a shady oak tree, was falling apart, with a broken limestone plaque revealing its mainly empty interior. The two-shelf, aboveground crypt had no coffins within, and maybe a few bone fragments and splintered wood debris lay on its caveau floor. This is not an uncommon sight in the older New Orleans cemeteries, so the tomb was not particularly noticeable in and of itself.

For quite some time I respectfully walked all the way around the area, nodding politely as I stepped around to give privacy. One day, while in haste during a cleanup, I neglected to take the side route and accidentally walked through this area without realizing it. I stopped dead in my tracks in the center to turn around. I felt something.

Oh—it's okay now, I thought.

The energy had totally changed. I said hello and went about my business.

It turned out, as time went by Richard would make sure I came over. He would shake the branches in the trees as a greeting and pitch acorns at me. I sat under the trees just to say hello. Sometimes I might sing a song or bring him a toy. I always brought him candy. I still do, even though he is not really here as often, for I helped him find a bit of trust and courage to travel on. At first, I did not realize he was a child. I did not pry or even try to connect out of courtesy. It became more and more clear as time went by.

I also did not realize that his happy spirit, who was in the tree when it shook, was the same spirit that I encountered in other areas showing up in quite a different form. Richard's spirit was in his happy, carefree mood while in the trees, but he was not only in the trees. Spirits can have moods, just like you and I.

For many years, a low-to-the-ground apparition would pass me by, accompanied by a distinct whooshing and squeaking sound of metal to pavement. It turns out this apparition was the same spirit as the boy in the tree! A few years of experiences, visuals, sounds, and multiple mediumship sessions with others at my side helped us figure it out. He did not speak, but a collective understanding telepathically deduced the traumas that Richard carried.

When Richard was free, he was in the tree and was safe as a growing spirit who could climb and play. But when he moved out of those boundaries, he was more of his ghost back in an archaic scoot of his crude moving device that he used in life, not a wheelchair. Richard scooted about, dragging his body behind him with his head tilted. When sending love to him in a group session, I had a doctor in my group one night. She understood the situation immediately. This doctor was not a psychic and she didn't need to be, for she was the right person at the right time to decipher all the signs, pictures, and apparitions. Richard recognized her talent and energies and gave her the full visual. Richard had cerebral palsy. The doctor was a specialist in this field. I had mistakenly thought Richard had polio prior to that. I later showed the doctor photographs and she pointed out Richard's tilted head in several of them. She explained that the unusual wheelchair-like device that I saw—a flat board with wheels—was what people with cerebral palsy would have used in the nineteenth century to get around.

I told the doctor about something incredible that Greg Avery of MUFON (Mutual UFO Network) and I had caught on video years before: an inexplicable flash of light—an apelike shadow with tentacle-like arms scooting low to the ground in superfast motion—accompanied by squeaking sounds, like old wheels. This was perfect Hollywood horror story material, and Greg was creeped out, but it had never bothered me. The energy was not at all malevolent. Unusual, yes; threatening, no. Since childhood, I always knew not to judge a book by its cover. I had not yet realized, though, that the two incarnations were the same spirit until this night. The doctor helped us finally understand what we'd seen.

Remember that nineteenth-century people with afflictions such as cerebral palsy were treated badly in life. They could be locked away, jeered at on the streets, and treated as if they were cursed. This was the life that Richard lived and learned. As a result, he did not have much trust in humankind. During one visit, I let him know that people's understanding of physical handicaps has changed for the better. He perked up when people came by on wheelchairs. I explained the Special Olympics to him. I also brought him gifts. I helped teach him a bit of trust.

All this, plus a little love and understanding, melted away the fears that originally projected that "stay away" force field that would have been misconstrued by many as a malevolent energy. More and more, Richard was manifesting as the happy boy in the trees. I prayed and helped him know there was possibly a better place, a different place he could go that he could trust. I also helped him know that his tree, or another tree he chose, would always be there for him, and this was a place he could come back to and climb whenever he wanted.

Richard had a hard life and he originally had no reason to trust too many humans, but we learned from each other and became friends. I do believe the love and understanding we shared awakened his spirit self to rest in peace. Love ya, Richard.

Harry

Harry is an interesting boy. For the first year or so that I saw, sensed, heard, and felt him, I did not know his name. He stays near a special tree. I believe it was a favorite tree in life as well as in afterlife. Harry would also pitch acorns at my head from the road if he wanted attention. This was sometimes followed by a whoosh of icy wind that sent my hair flying. He consistently put visuals in people's heads that came near—images of canoes, rope swings, and playing ball. He was a tall, lanky twelve-year-old who appears much older, more like a young man of sixteen or seventeen. He sometimes shows up on a limb of his tree wearing rolled-up blue jeans and a straw hat, with legs swinging freely—very Huck Finn in look and time period.

I brought Harry a straw hat. I brought him a ball that he would somehow secretly throw with an invisible pitch while we were standing nearby. There were at least a dozen times that various men I was with heard their names called by a little boy long before I mentioned anything about Harry. But again, at first I did not know his name was Harry. A lady asked me his name one day, and I confessed that I did not know. I felt remiss for not having inquired earlier.

"Hello. My name is Mary. What's yours?" I announced as I bent down to place an offering at the roots of his tree.

I heard an inner answer right away: *Harry*.

A dumb thought popped into my head right at that moment: *Harry doesn't sound like a kid's name*. Then my phone rang. Broken out of my trance, I glanced at my phone. A midwestern number I didn't recognize. I turned the ringer off so I could proceed with my mission, and I started to leave with a small group behind me when the phone rang again. I took it out of my purse and glanced at it. Same number. How persistent! I turned the ringer off again. I continued to walk away. The phone rang a third time. This time my phone vibrated, indicating I had a voice message. Someone was forcing his or her way through. My curiosity was piqued. I decided we should listen to the message. It was a little boy's voice, and all he said was, "Hello, my name is Harry." Click.

Through the powers of Spirit and Harry's spirit acting through a little boy whose voice had not changed yet, my inner psychic clairaudience was validated. Synchronicity!

He answers to Harry. This also solved the age-old question of Harry's age. The voice on the phone was a young boy whose voice had not changed yet. Harry always gravitated to grown men. He pulled at facial hair and arm hair—things he had not yet acquired in life. He was tall for his age when he died, but he was still a kid bordering on adolescence. He wanted a playmate and a big brother/father-like figure.

I brought my son Jagger to climb the tree and to sit under it with his Game Boy so Harry could watch. We invited Harry to one of Jagger's birthday parties, and I have pictures of an energy trail and orbs following us to the car.

Harry also wanted to have his story told. He was not buried in that graveyard, and his body was never found. Harry lay somewhere in Lake Pontchartrain. His rope swing and canoe imagery led us to put the pieces together: He had drowned. Once the full story was out, a little girl spirit started to appear near Harry. She was quiet and seemingly just out of his reach. We could see Harry and her, but they couldn't seem to see each other, though they were just feet apart. She was his rescue and escort, coming to get him. I did as much as I could to get them together. I explained to both of them what I thought was going on. I explained to Harry that this would always be his tree house.

He took leave of his daily tree climb. She was his sister, and I helped them get together so they could walk off into the sunset. The time and constant imagery of water, canoes, and rope swings are, alas, now few and far between. Harry comes back once in a while to play, but rarely. Why? Because he can. He and many spirits can come and go freely and enjoy the wonders of their lives, visit friends and family, and watch over us. I still bring him treats, books, and tell his tale—for that tree is Harry's headstone and this is Harry's legacy. Rest in peace, Harry.

The Lady in White

New Orleans owns a beautiful hitchhiking ghost wearing a wedding dress. She frantically hails a cab near the cemetery gates. The cabbie takes her to fetch her sick child, and she disappears without paying. The angry cabbie pursues his fare and is greeted by a grieving father who just moments before lost his child. Last year, he lost his wife; he buried her in her wedding dress.

Tales such as these have grown to join the ranks of urban legend. But do urban legends start from source material? Are they actual experiences passed down for generations? Maybe they can be borrowed folklore, refitted and redesigned for the times and locales they hitchhike to. But folklore is not just fiction. It defines a people and an era.

Consider that they are real.

Countless eyewitness reports say that certain ancestors come in to help escort the passing of their loved ones. Rarely would they be in need of a taxi, but spirits that hitchhike can be both a literal and metaphoric phenomenon. Sometimes they do an astral tagalong to transport.

There are many tales of literal hitchhiking spirits on the roads the world over. This is the particular story passed down to me as a child. No one ever really identified the cemetery. I heard from some people that this occurred around New Orleans's Cemetery District in Mid-City, where fifteen graveyards line a crossroads. Others have said it was one of the St. Louis cemeteries. I have also even heard that she was in front of the old Girod Street Cemetery.

For this particular tale, I cannot verify the whos and wheres, but I can verify my own lady in white—a wandering spirit in her wedding dress floating between tombs in our Cemetery District.

Nature takes its toll on our old tombs; grave robbers may take the rest, and even the homeless have a hand in the destruction. If a family is gone and no one is left to maintain the plot, or if there is no official perpetual care set up and only family care remains, a plaque could fall off due to lack of mortar and crumbling brick. With the assistance of homeless vagrants seeking shelter or grave robbers seeking pilfer, thousands of old tombs are damaged. It was said that it was the homeless that were the downfall of our old Girod Street Cemetery that closed in 1957 due to massive disrepair.

I have seen all of these things occur. I have sealed a few tombs back up personally. I have locked some homeless out of their shantytowns built in cemeteries by installing new gates and monitoring the grounds. I have even personally reburied scattered remains. But these naturally decayed monuments standing proud in all the graveyards of New Orleans have also become a natural history course with revealing architectural decay, teaching from beyond the grave. The aging also exposes beautiful antique coffins of iron or simple ones of crumbling wooden boxes filled with bones— some even rather well dressed.

Coffins fall apart before the skin comes off your bones, and the skin comes off your bones before the clothes come off your back—hence, my lady in white. Walking between tombs near an area where she was buried, my lady in white just wanders, says nothing. Splintered wood shards of a caved-in coffin accompanied by a white flash of silk and bone can be seen from outside her opened tomb.

I researched many witnesses to her beautiful fading dress, seen in various stages of decay over the years. A New Orleans policeman, a local cemetery sexton, and everyday local visitors shared their tales. This tattered, but beautiful aging white silk wedding dress, with limp lace frills, slightly yellowed with time, dressed her remains in an old coffin. There was a bit of beading and sequin gild hanging on for dear life that occasionally caught the light just right and spotlighted her tomb. It was an obvious display for all to see who walked near. It seems her wedding dress was made to last and lovingly adorned her singing bones.

Though her spirit sightings lasted for several years, she was eventually sealed back up. Doug Nellums, cemetery caretaker, sealed her up himself, still with her dress covering her remains, and my phantom lady vanished, content, for a while.

Several years later, she began to walk again. Recognizing this spectral beauty, I pursued her lead, thinking something must be wrong. I followed her cue, walked into a cemetery, and turned a corner near her row. There I saw her tomb had been disturbed once again. Upon looking in, there were no more bones to be seen, and certainly no beautiful faded wedding dress—no lace, no beads. Just an old empty splintered box.

If she wandered at first simply to point the way to the disturbance of yesteryear and now walked again to inform about the desecration at hand, imagine how she could haunt those who took her bones. I said prayers and tossed a rose in the vault for her spirit. This sepulcher was sealed yet again, and she wanders no more.

It was not uncommon to be buried in one's wedding dress. I know not if my lady in white has anything to do with our original ghost-that-takes-a-taxi tale, but it's possible.

The Crossroads

My earliest childhood memories are within the cemetery gates. The cemeteries were normal weekend jaunts with my grandma since I was a baby. I was told the ancestors' tales with words of love whispered between tears and Hail Marys to a backbeat of clanking rosary beads in hand, tapping on the limestone nearby. I was taught it was good manners to nod and simply say hello as we wandered near tombs. Toys and food were left near the stoops of many crypts, and pretty flowers, freshly gifted, brilliantly offset the gray and added life to the graveyards. I was taught that the toys were for the "little angels" to play with, food was to feed them, and it was plain courtesy to bring in things that they had enjoyed in life.

Many children would play quietly in the graveyards back in the day. As I got older, many of us branched out to roam through all fifteen neighboring cemeteries and played hide-and-seek. On these journeys, I discovered personal notes, wrapped gifts, and articles of clothing set out on the tombs. Even handmade altars and holiday décor were evident. I saw people talking, singing, and sometimes screaming at their buried loved ones; occasionally, spirits were at their sides, looking over them.

I still roam these same cemeteries now and connect with the heart and souls of New Orleans. Yet, flowers are just not as plentiful, families are not seen as often, and the children of the flesh are absent.

I drive through this Cemetery District two or three times per day. This three-way crossroads is my neighborhood. I have friends and family in each and every one.

One day, as I was crossing through, I was forced to brake hard to avoid hitting a person who jumped in front of the car seemingly out of nowhere. But it was too late. That person was dead, and long before I came near him. His ghost just vanished. I was relieved. Others in my neighborhood note similar phenomena.

Occasionally, people in period clothing and out of time stroll across the street or disappear through cemetery walls.

There is an inordinate amount of accidents with people who don't turn at all at the foot of Canal Street and plow right through the heavy iron fence as if it just isn't there. This is a major crossroads, a threshold of the living and the dead. People just keep driving, straight into Greenwood Cemetery. But is it a burst to get through or get out? It seems that this very well lit and overt monumental cemetery right in front of their face must somehow simply slip away, or maybe something just jumps in front of them and they lose control.

Every year, as part of a ceremonial crossroads clearing around Easter, I cleanse and feed that crossroads at its center point. This has seriously reduced the number of accidents there which had dramatically increased after Katrina. Maybe drivers lose control as phantom pedestrians stroll by; or real-world dangers of DUIs factor into the mix of accidents here; but I will continue to spiritually cleanse that area for the rest of my days.

Underneath Us All

There are many areas in New Orleans where hidden cemeteries live under our buildings and streets. Both plague and foul play could make quick, clandestine burials a necessity in any old nook or cranny in town. We pass atop them every single day. New Orleans is notorious for building on top of cemeteries, with full knowledge that bodies are still buried below. Courtyard landscaping finds are more than old bottles down under in concealed wells. Contractors come up with literal skeletons in closets. The list of locations for forgotten or overgrown cemeteries continues to surprise us, mainly proving that here in New Orleans, we are not far removed from our ancestors' presence. Nice dry, pumped land was far too valuable of a commodity here. If you didn't claim your property, as in your departed family members' remains, they could be left behind. The cemetery might be sold off, lot by lot, and built over.

At least two blocks of the French Quarter are built on top of old cemeteries. The old Girod Street Protestant Cemetery, originally known as *"cimetière des hérétiques,"* was mostly relocated, but some of it still lies below the Superdome parking lot. A section of I-10 and West End Boulevard is supported by tens of thousands of dead Irish Catholics who perished while digging the "Old" Basin Canal below. A grammar school and playground uptown is built atop another. Three blocks of Canal Boulevard conceal Cypress Grove Cemetery No. 2, plus random neighborhoods pop up surprise cadavers all over town.

A prime example of a defunct cemetery is the somewhat forgotten St. Peter Street Cemetery. It officially ended its reign in 1789 with the advent of a newer aboveground St. Louis Cemetery. But for a few years prior and a few years after, both cemeteries were continuously used in the transition.

In June 2011, I was walking down the block, sweaty and hot on a typical New Orleans humid summer day. I saw two buildings with a banner stretched between them saying MARCELLO PROPERTIES. Vincent Marcello had been my landlord for years, and I knew him and many of his construction workers. I saw a familiar face but still addressed him as I would a stranger when I watchdog French Quarter construction:

"Hey, got any bones back there?"

"Yeah, Mary. Come on in the back."

"Oh shit." I suddenly realized where I was standing.

"Well, I guess you do have bones back there."

I was standing inside that old St. Peter Street Cemetery. The foreman, Phil, escorted me through the construction zone and laid out the plans. "Vincent is putting a lot of care into this project. We removed the brick wall separating the two buildings' courtyards to make one large one. We're taking up the old flagstones over there; we're digging a lap pool. That's where we got 'em."

A section that was not very large was cordoned off for the pool.

I was told that the LSU Archaeology Department and the Vieux Carré Commission had already been on the scene. The Commission watches the historical integrity of the buildings in the historic French Quarter. Vincent personally called in the LSU Osteoarchaeology Department to offer them the chance to work with the remains. I learned then what the law is: When you dig down more than three feet, you have to move the bodies.

Now, mind you, there are many more hundreds of square feet besides the small section for the pool, all with coffins and remains below; but those did not need to be moved. After all, they weren't digging everywhere. I was also informed that they had already found coffins, pipes, ceramics, and various assorted sundries on the initial dig. It would be a few months before they would actually remove the coffins for the pool. I was concerned about how the spirit disruption would affect everything. I also requested to be present when they disinterred the remains. I figured I'd better do something quick, since they had just started breaking ground.

My goal was to protect the living and the dead. I wanted no trouble for the crew, plus in a situation like this, a spiritual touch was necessary. I had a few things with me for this purpose: holy water, Florida water, holy oil, tobacco, Spanish moss, candy, and some rum. I also had a sacred amulet and a gator tooth. I proceeded to pray and informed the spirits that if any of them were still attached to the bodies and could hear me, they were going to be moved. I explained what was going to happen, where they were going, and why. I also let them know they would be reburied eventually. I explained that the secrets that lay within their bones might help the medical profession and hence someone else in the future. They would also help correct history for diet, disease, osteopathic deformities, race, and many other things that have been documented by archaeologists while examining the disinterred remains from our past.

I asked the spirits to be gentle to the workers, for they mean them no harm. They would just be rebuilding the buildings that had been on top of them for several centuries. I prayed for this, and for the spirits, and thanked them for their cooperation. I sprinkled Florida water so any possible negative vibrations would be settled, and made the sign of the cross with holy water and oil on the ground. I gave them sweets and rum smudged with the smoke and said another prayer to close the gates. Then I went on my way.

The removal of the coffins took longer than expected. By then, I was already on a more ancient archaeological and European sacred-site exploration of my own. Upon my return, I found out the pool had been dug and the bodies were now in LSU's Osteo-archaeology Department in Baton Rouge.

I drove by one night on a private outing with a couple. One of Vincent's foremen, Phil, was standing outside the building. I pulled over.

"Hey, I heard that you removed a lot of coffins and they were still in one piece." This was amazing considering the last burials were around 1789. That original cypress wood here can really take a beating.

"Yeah, we took fifteen out in all, and many were below them, but we did not have to move those since we weren't digging deeper," Phil replied.

"Wow."

"Yeah. We found so many artifacts and shards of ceramics in the old well that the archaeologists were taking them out by the wheelbarrow full. We turned that well into a hot tub!

"There's still two coffins back there now," Phil said.

"Can we see?" I asked.

"Sure."

As we walked in, I asked, "Did you have any trouble with hauntings during the excavation or construction?"

"No, not at all," Phil said. "Thank you so much for doing what you did. We had no hauntings, no trouble whatsoever. In fact, everything went unusually smooth."

"Good! I'm glad the spirits are at rest."

They did indeed feel at ease as we entered the premises. We walked toward the back, down the alley, past the brick walls, and into the newly renovated courtyard.

Phil was describing the detailed work he had done, while I was making a beeline for the pool to take a picture of the coffins.

I expected to see a partially completed lap pool with a couple of old coffins stacked nearby. I did not. The lap pool was completely filled with water, had a slightly textured bottom, and was backlit—everything was totally complete.

"Phil, where are the coffins?" I asked.

He was busy pointing out the restoration accomplishments to my guests but absent-mindedly said, "In the pool, Mary."

"In the pool?" What the hell? The pool was completely filled. Like an idiot, I bent over to stare down deeply into the water. What were the coffins doing, swimming?

"Phil, what are you talking about?"

"Oh, sorry."

He came closer to where I was standing and pointed me to the right.

"You see? Over there. The steps. We decided to just leave the last two coffins in place and make the steps into the pool out of them. See, look."

Those steps were slightly irregular in size and shape and perfectly covered over with a nice cement pour—an ingenious method. They just covered over those two coffins so as not to dislocate them. In that pool, you tiptoe over the dead before you swim over the dead. Only in New Orleans.

By early 2015, the LSU Osteoarchaeology Department had finished with their studies on the remains, and on April 18 that year, a great second-line jazz funeral escorted these citizens with full Catholic ritual blessings and reburied their remains in St. Louis Cemetery No. 1 in the recycled Portuguese Society tomb courtesy of the Archdiocese of New Orleans.

The Bronze Beauty

New Orleans boasts the first legalized red-light district: Storyville was active from 1898 to 1917. The District's most famous madam, in this most scandalous of sin cities, will always be Josie Arlington. Thousand-dollar bottles of champagne flowed from her brothel. Her house was the crème de la crème, the most exclusive in the entire Tenderloin District, where she reigned as queen.

Madam Josie Arlington retired from the public eye, defeated, in 1909. She moved into her private mansion on Esplanade Avenue in the Fauborg St. John tormented with the fear of the fire that had nearly claimed her life a few years prior and spun her into a morbid melancholy. Was Josie still working inside those walls, or was she just the haunted recluse as others claim? Josie Arlington, born Mary Anna Deubler, died only five years later on Valentines Day 1914 and moved again. This time into her exquisite new red-marble resting place that she designed in 1911 to be built in the richest cemetery in North America—Metairie Cemetery.

Soon after Josie's burial, throngs of people gathered around her marble mansion of last repose. It seems the tomb glowed red around sunset, flickering ever so, with crimson marble flames perched perfectly atop, somehow saying she was still in that eternal red-light district down below. More and more people would gather at twilight time, some bickering back and forth about if the now-known "Flaming Tomb" was truly paranormal. The family was embarrassed, and the cemetery was embarrassed, but it was not as if they didn't know of the Madam's legacy.

Ten years after her death, it was claimed that Josie Arlington's tomb was sold to a relative, supposedly out of embarrassment, but more likely, out of financial need. Forced inheritance of tombs is the norm here, but they said Josie was disinterred and secretly moved. My archive research differs from rumor, for there is no record of tomb sale or disinterment of her body. A little girl, Catherine, did join her in 1924, but it seems Josie was, at best, moved only down to the ossuary/caveau below.

The red glow of the flaming tomb actually extinguished itself simultaneously with this exchange. The skeptics said nearby stoplight was always to blame for the scarlet hue. Others said that couldn't be the source because of the angle of the stoplight and its distance from the tomb, but the red light was moved when Josie was, so the mystery remains.

Yet a new phenomenon emerged around this same time, for Josie would not be forgotten. Cemetery sextons began noticing an even more peculiar paranormal sight, for Josie seemed still not at rest and needed to claim her fame. There is an iron maiden statue forever knocking at the tomb door—this statue, actually cast in bronze, began to walk all by itself. Several generations of workers have watched this beautiful bronze woman trudging through the cemetery grounds, weary and haggard and all alone, with her skirt puddling behind. She makes her way through the grounds, eventually returning to her rightful tomb. She proceeds to climb up the cold, hard marble stairs and reaches for the thick bronze door knocker. Then a deafening pounding ensues—*Bang! Bang! Bang!*—echoing throughout the cemetery, announcing her return. Mind you, this is not a shadow or shade of this bronze beauty, but a statue of more than five hundred pounds, walking in a never-ending quest to enter that door that seems to refuse reentry evermore.

The statue itself has a threefold meaning. This beautiful iron maiden, in her continuous search, clasps a bouquet of thirteen bronze roses holding an interesting mystery. It is a fact that Josie was very particular about whom she would hire in her house. Josie was steadfast that no girl was ever to be deflowered in her care, even though virgins were a popular commodity to be auctioned off inside other Storyville brothels. Only those seasoned in the erotic arts were allowed through her Tenderloin door—not too young and not too old. Virgins need not apply. So they are left forever knocking.

A second meaning goes more to the heart of the matter. One fateful night, a young Josie stayed out a bit too late for her family's liking. When she knocked on the door of her family home late that evening, she was turned away. Josie pounded throughout the night, but to no avail, and thus she began her life on the streets. She was only thirteen. She eventually did quite well for herself. The licenses for New Orleans's ladies of the night were issued for "fast, lewd and abandoned women."

But now, I have found this beautiful statue holds a third meaning. The deafening pounding occurs only after her spirit cemetery sojourn and return are done. From a secret burial spot, she roams in vain, just to be turned away from her rightful resting place. Eternally, she's denied entry again and again. Author Lyle Saxon claims that there was no red light anywhere near the tomb at the time, and reports that if neighbors call to complain about the infernal banging of metal on metal throughout the night, they are simply told, "Oh, that's just the maiden trying to get in."

But could a statue such as this really walk by itself? Has it ever actually been seen en route? The knocking sound is more easily understood, but anything is possible. One time, that bronze beauty was found off its tomb on the edge of the cemetery near the walking gate. Another time it was found lying facedown by Bayou St. John two miles away. These spots were en route to Josie's private home on the other side of the bayou.

Her spirit is aware, and anomalies such as orbs and ectoplasm appear around her tomb. She would not have to be within this fine sepulcher for her spirit to still claim its due. Sounds of parties and clinking glasses have been heard by strangers at my side visiting over the years, and the general feeling of revelry has been felt by those who have no idea whose tomb it is. Josie still loves to come out for parties.

I hold personal evidence of Josie's residuals remaining in her private residence. I formally invited Josie as the first guest to the grand reopening party in her newly restored former home.

"Hear the jazz," "See the girls," "Relive the days of Storyville," and other phrases were written on the invite for that particular soirée. But an earlier, unexpected wedding reception slipped through onto the premises prior to my big bash, and the other party seemed to be one conjured up by Josie's hand. This party seemed to prefer swing to jazz and came with a bang, not a whimper. The queen of Storyville came to that party and brought an unexpected X-rated theme along with her.

The mansion had been moved physically from its original Esplanade site long ago, which may have awakened our dear madam. When interior renovations began again, this perhaps reinforced guardianship of Josie's watch further—that, and the promise of a party. I wonder if she haunts the old Esplanade address as well as the physical building's new location.

Josie seems to get out and about, and her own red light still flickers softly, but occasionally her personal pulsing red beam triggers a few primal instincts from the other side.

✦

The Spirits' Who's Who

- **Josie as Party Planner**—Spirits who help execute and plan the party. Josie still enjoys this starring role when champagne is served, and she was the (after)life of at least one party I know of. Most of us wear many hats.

- **Josie as Restless Spirit**—An unsettled spirit who has unfulfilled longings and is in constant search of filling his or her emptiness. Madame Josie Arlington could be constantly searching for her rightful resting spot, whether that's in her tomb or in her old home. That unplanned move out of her final resting place triggered a deeper longing as her unsatisfied soul part awoke when she was booted out of her tomb. A living statue, constantly searching, constantly knocking and not gaining entrance, was a recurring metaphor in Josie's life and a somewhat "set in bronze" theme for her afterlife.

- **Josie as Sex Therapist**— On a lighter note, Josie may have a little sway in the bedroom. Ask her advice, see what happens.

- **Playmate**—Groups of happy spirit children do still play together in the park, the trees, and the cemeteries. They are sometimes triggered when I bring groups of young school-age children in on field trips. They are generally happy, lively, and just want to have fun. They grasp the opportunity to tag along and revel in the energy of like-age humans.

- **Sentry**—A spirit who polices a location. My shadow man was a sentry for the cemetery, and when he recognized that I too was a kindred sentry, he eventually trusted me and became an ally. This particular shadow soul also became a protector for me personally. This mission eventually helped him evolve and find self-worth and a purpose.

- **Shadow Person**—This is a human-shaped ghost that looks like a dark shadow. They are very private and shy and try to hide in between things to avoid human contact, and they don't seek communication. I believe they get a bad rap. Shadow people are not evil, like others say. That shadow's smell could have been a warning, but I took it as a message. It was also a test. That olfactory sense is an archaic one, and a powerful trigger. Common paranormal clairscents include perfumes, cigar smoke, or the familiar smell of a loved one. The smell can be a nasty one.

- **Talking Bones**—Were those bones I talked to in the pool just bones, or were they spirits inside their perfect cypress coffins? Does it matter? I fulfilled my duty to pray and to protect both the living and the dead. Sometimes bones are just bones, and sometimes bones have stories to share. Some are alive. Osteo-archaeologists deal in the quantitative work with bones. Others, like me, do the qualitative studies. Both are important. I prefer to put the humanness and the spirit back in "dem bones" and believe they are all holy relics. I also believe in the supernatural connection as well as genetic memory—both can be communicated.

- **Teacher**—Children's spirits can also be great teachers and are a reminder of the simple needs in life to be content: love, trust, and even play. The children spirits I mentioned also helped specific people reflect on what they needed to see in their own lives.

✦

Afterlife Lessons

Knock three times as you enter a cemetery or sacred site. This is out of respect and it relays the message of honorable intentions. Bring a gift, be sincere, and always ask permission as you walk through the threshold. Introduce yourself and your purpose. The spirits taught me directly, and my family taught me directly.

There are "in-between lives" talked about, along with the common belief in past lives, future lives, and so on. There is spirit counseling that can occur during these in-between times, along with a form of ancestral guardianship we can share.

Not all paranormal occurrences are visual. All the senses are involved, and not everyone picks up the same things at the same time in the same way. It is about both the sender and the receiver's capabilities. Clairsentience (touch) is the most common paranormal ability; clairaudience (sound) is second; clairscent (smell) is third; and last is clairvoyance (sight).

I have learned that some spirits only want to speak to one specific person, and not everyone present will connect with the same spirit in the same way. It can be like piecing together a puzzle: Each step, fitted correctly, reveals the next pieces' correct positions. Take the time and trust the process.

Pay attention to signs, changes in moods, and photographs, too, for their synchronicity is part of the message experience. This simultaneous stimulus alongside other anomalous occurrences is meaningful, not simple coincidence.

If you are to tap into the multidimensional worlds that we live in every day, everywhere, you need to learn to let go, let it flow, and trust the signs, information, and your own intuition.

It is best to face our own traumas in life and get clear, but children may not always have had time. Children who led happy lives have easier transitions. No worries, in general, most children spirits are not lost; they just seem to want recess over here.

Not all children spirits died young, but many did. If childhood was their happiest time or most emotional time, spirits could choose to wear that suit and return to relive that form. But if they grew up to adulthood, and had careers and families of their own, they could also appear to their spouses, children, or coworkers in different attire.

Residual energy can be somewhat of an advantage, but sometimes it may affect people adversely. For example, places with a history of fights, anger, or violent death could have problematic residual energies to contend with. In Josie's case, there is perhaps more sexual energy than you can swallow.

Check your ego in life. Make sure that when you are near your way out, at least by your eleventh hour, your life is in order. If you cling too hard to life, it may thwart your spiritual journey.

Warnings

Pay respect.

Close the gates behind you.

Don't judge a book by its cover.

Renovation could wake the dead anywhere, but special caution should be taken when doing so in locales that were graveyards. Address the original builder or those who have lain there before. Salute them and thank them for sharing their space, and announce your intentions. This could soothe away any misunderstandings before they start. Remember, to the spirits it could look like you are destroying things. And if you happen to ever move over an old graveyard or buy a used tomb, remember to do the same plus pray for them and perform a little extra cleansing, too.

Lagniappe

Katrina and the *Cauchemar*

J UST WHEN I THOUGHT the evil was dormant after Hurricane
Katrina, an icy wind broke the calm stillness of slumber on
a sweltering July night. My bleary eyes opened to a billowy,
ethereal ripple cascading phantasmagorically at my side. This entity
tore through the thin veil that separates my precarious existence
from the other side. My once meticulously protected dimension,
which I admittedly live on the edge of, had been breached!

"Not again," I sighed. But this particular unearthly presence
startled even my supernormal sight: its Hollywood attire, complete with floating sheet, was very strange. Before I could react,
I was paralyzed as its menacing cackle echoed its evil in my ears.
This, of course, removed any lingering vestiges of what is normally
known as sleep and reminded me yet again not to be so com-
placent in the comfort of such indulgences. Normally, this early
ethereal warning should have proved enough time for my battle

mode to kick into gear, but it pounced with incredible speed and reach. An inner scream welled up in me but would not—could not—release.

How unlike me, I pondered, as one thought after another raced by at an alarming rate, all the while attempting to release the scream trapped within. *I was trained for this—I can win this battle.*

Then the realization sunk in: *I can't move my body.* But my mind was strong and alert, and I could move my eyes. I looked up to see where the liquid curtain did its vaporous veil dance, and I could now see a very small but distinct portal from which emanated its unearthly male vibrato. This deep, resonating, yet hollow tone of a vaguely familiar attempt at a laugh echoed through the room. Something wasn't quite right about it all.

It reached toward me from there, and through there it need return!

But wait. Laughter is listed as a weapon to destroy some monsters. There sure had been a drought of laughter here since the storm. But that didn't really seem to be the right weapon of choice. This warranted more of the gym coach effect: To embarrass a weakling into shipshape required submission, humiliation, and an extra plunge, a twist of the knife to deflate it. There was no time for psychic debate or negotiation, not with this one. But laughter was now on my list and an ace up my sleeve.

Even after the past year of post-Katrina encounters with many dark sorts that were unleashed since the deluge, I was still unsure what I was actually fighting. But I knew why: I was fighting for the survival of my whole town! Whoever or whatever this is, it is a predator.

I had robbed a lot of food from this one, not only in my own home, but in other ways around my whole hometown in the past year of combat. This cycle for battle mode returned, and maybe with more power this year. It was voracious in its cycle now.

When I was attacked the previous year, IT showed itself in its natural raw state, with no anthropomorphic attire at all. So why did this choose to pick a sheet out of my brain now? How odd. IT was not intelligent, but IT was set free. IT might not be able to be classified as classically evil, but somehow worse: amoral and primordial, a much more difficult adversary.

It had a false, humanoid tone; weak, but still sinister. It was like canned laughter from a bad sitcom. I knew it sounded familiar, and then I realized—this mimicking laugh was a recording!

And I am also familiar with these types of attacks. Many called it "ridden by a hag." Here in Louisiana, this is *cauchemar*. Was this one at hand really a mere *cauchemar*? No. I think it functions more like a childlike spawn, or worker bee who returns to the queen mother with food. So, this spawn was part of a much larger being. If I weakened it, maybe I could weaken the whole.

I was aware or afraid that the recent quiet times were no true indicator that the original mother beast was slain. It was more like a hibernating or gestating opponent, at best. But this one at hand had to be dealt with in the now, and I just may have identified an Achilles heel.

It was hungry and looking for food, but so was I. Katrina had put everyone into a panic state of lack; there was still famine lurking in the long road to the recovery of New Orleans. The cupboard was bare, and no one else best dare come threaten my family, the city, or my children. There had been too much looting all around for the eye to see, and I'd be damned if I was part of the menu. A vigilante mode was a side option offered now on everyone's plate; it was either choose that or choose to be a victim. I would never be a victim. It was up to me to show IT what I was made of.

The analytical mind stirred again as I calculated the facts. The vortex was still open; I could see it. This thing could be reversed, but the direction of my energy was diverted and busy trying to break this hold. What really mattered now was that I had the ability to see this entry at its exact location and reverse it through the same.

The space it emitted through was apparent—just a two-inch circle at best. More of these beings might come through simply because they could! However, since this was a port of debarkation as well, I could maneuver it all back through, even if it was one spirit at a time.

Struggling inside with all my strength, I tried to move in vain. The madder I got, the stronger I got. Fury was my winged avenger, called forth to my side. *Why. Can't. I. Scream?!*

I knew what was going on. I knew something was trying to get inside me. I have battled these things before, taught about them, studied them since I was twelve years old, when I got a glimpse of the shadow side of the spirit worlds. The anger, boiling and seething, was now welling up inside me, ready to erupt. Fighting through with all my might, I brought the scream up from deep within myself: *"Aghhhhhhhh!"*

I twitched and contorted and roared as the lion echoes through the ether, calling every spirit and power of the almighty up for an army as I broke free from the trap. I startled myself with the unfamiliar sound of my own scream. How dare this being come into my domain and penetrate the protections I so carefully rebuilt?

I began to banish: "Don't even try to shoot me down, not now. You have no right. You dare to sup upon my vital energy? I was here first, and I fought through hell to find my way back. So just stay away, monster. I am not afraid of you. Leave me be. Damn looter. Scavenger. Trying to take what you can't earn on you own. No, you are worse—*imposter*."

The anger gave way to even more power, and I now mustered my true voice and began to banish further and bind with all my might. I turned that scream into a turbine force and slammed its chicken-shit ass right against the wall, paralyzing it.

"I will destroy you now, you puny piece of slime. Out of my life, out of my home, away from my family, and out of this town! Be gone, you worthless demon spawn—*Hahahahaha*!

"Go . . . leave now. In the name of Jesus, I rebuke you. With the power of the loa and the light and the strength of Michael the Archangel and all the archangels, I rebuke you. Go down, deep into the pit and stay! You foul, pathetic, miserable excuse for existence, be gone! You can't even laugh correctly on your own. Go crawl back and find your master, your mother demon! Go—seek your kindred kind and leave this space! Leave this time! Be gone! Be gone!"

Its flaccid form shrank further as it was swallowed back through that two-inch portal from whence it came. The door slammed shut and it evaporated in a flash. I snapped up with all of my movement and senses and looked around the room. It was done!

Was this really the first time I was truly trapped, even temporarily? It was certainly not the first, but the first in more than forty years. This made me mad. It took a moment to muster all my strength. I moved my mouth and heard myself whisper, "Monster."

I began to wonder why this particular creature had come. I had done so many cleansings and had put so many new protections and fortifications in and around my home. In fact, I had put them all over the entire city. I guess now it was time for even more.

I turned to check on my husband nearby. He seemed untouched, unaware. This both calmed and angered me. I leapt out of bed to go check on my child. There I found my mamma kitty, Bast, standing guard at his door. She was protecting my innocent Jagger, who was twelve at the time. She had been guarding him diligently as of late.

Some of the symptoms of this intruder fit perfectly in the folklore indwellers occupying our swamps, where hordes of wild monsters fed strong through all the fears that this town, besieged by storms, seemed to populate. Sometimes folklore is real; post-Katrina was one of those times.

Katrina unleashed something more archaic than just this annoying intruder. There was *IT*. IT was what I call this mammoth mother haint, but tonight's entity was just its little minion *cauchemar* sent out aforaging. I had been battling IT for over a year, but I knew I had many more battles yet to come. It was time for the big guns.

We had so very few spirits here after Katrina. Our watchers, the ancestors, and the architects that guard this town were stripped from their posts. My simple explanation is that our spirits evacuated with their families, but this was not a simple situation. Our spirit allies were somehow captured, making New Orleans a ghost town of a different variety. This left us very vulnerable, for without these watchers we were easy targets. Since they were gone, the dark side was set free. IT was big, dark, and extremely difficult to tame. It was my job to fight IT back, and it was IT's job to stop me.

I fought to the end. It took three long years to drive that darkness back, and it wasn't pretty, not pretty at all. While doing that, I also helped reinstate our guardian spirits back to their posts and became a midwife of New Orleans's spirit rebirth over the past decade!

I had the help of an army of living, healing warriors from many faiths spread out in a web across this continent. I also had

The Katrina Memorial built atop the old Charity Hospital cemetery in New Orleans commemorates many of our forgotten dead heroes.
Photo by Bloody Mary © BMT, Inc.

the help of an army of spirits, loas, angels, and even some interesting, previously unknown life-form helpers emerge from many multidimensional worlds to aid in the rescue.

New Orleans is safe again from IT, for now. There was a seed of knowledge and a rooting of transformation I planted within IT before I drove IT back. Now IT knows a little something more about the human race besides how it tastes.

The Spirits' Who's Who

- **Ancestors**—Protectors of your bloodline who have a vested interest in watching and helping their children and their children's children flourish and grow. Remember to send love their way. They are your actual immediate family plus maybe your God-family.

- **Angels**—Some can be quite fierce and come through with dramatic entries, not always with apparent wings. These particular angels crashed through a mirror to assist. One was very busy documenting information and was friendly, while the others were harried and just wanted to attend to the business at hand—very no-nonsense. The category of "Powers" fits here best as they were keepers of history and warrior angels. My previous angelic encounters have been less dramatic, but a consistent element of administrative queries and recording data are present. Some have been nurturing. Some have had wings.

- **Architects**—A group of spirit adepts, both celestial and ascended masters from various time periods of evolution. They provide great protection here. They arrived in groups of two and came forward in times of drastic changes and needs. They are like a board of directors who are divine architects/ healers.

- *Cauchemar*—This is a nightmare from the swamps. These hags press down on you to get every last drop of your vital energy. Their rumored preference is to sup on the energy of young men, all alone, in the night.

- **Familiars**—Usually referred to as an invisible guard or a physical assistant to mystics, whose familiars could be animals or humanoids. It is not uncommon that one of your pets would assume this role—a pet that has certain supernatural endowments. Your living pets love you, and many are willing to offer themselves to protect you and your family. You may note one of your pets seems different from the rest. They are intuitive and can indeed guide and guard you. I have one specific familiar cat in the flesh and one familiar dog in spirit now. These familiars are different from your totem animal spirit guides or your ghost pets.

- **Primordial**—That which feeds to survive with no discernable palate. They devour, divide, and conquer. Some may refer to this as a demon or a vampire.

- **Watchers**—Protectors and guardians who guard over your city or town; they work for the spirit of place.

Afterlife Lessons

Honor the spirit worlds, your protectors. Embrace the spirit guardians and acknowledge their importance, for when they are gone you won't know what hit you. Be strong in your beliefs. Remember to give thanks, and remember where you come from.

Take care and care-take.

✦

Warnings

Intuition is important, so trust your gut. Remember that this is your plane, so defend your rights. Be prepared, and if in battle mode, expect surprise attacks. Leave your fear behind.

Spirits generally come from a more celestial realm, back down to us through a sort of antenna, and we need to look up more often. Occasionally, a portal opens at eye level. But we have to look down, way down, below our radar, too. Some things creep up from the subterranean levels, just as IT did. Be aware.

6

Marie Laveau,
Queen of Voodoo

*Marie Laveau was setting in a rocking chair. She had a veil
on her head and a black-and-red shawl on her shoulders. It
looked like she had something in her lap that she was holding,
but I could not see what it was. She had a black skirt or dress
on. She did not seem unhappy; she seemed content. The other
woman was wearing a long white dress and smiling. She had
long dark hair and her left hand was on Marie's right shoulder. The person behind them was either dressed all in black or
was just in the shadows, or maybe even a shadow person. I
could not see what she or he looked like or why this person was
standing behind them. Then I saw you, Bloody Mary, just as
clear as clear can be. You just appeared in front of everyone,
which was something to behold!*

—Rob Icenhour to the author, May 23, 2012

Under the Claiborne bridge, in the Treme neighborhood, lives fabulous folk art focusing on many famous African Creole traditions and residents. Visitors to one of the entrances will be greeted by the mural of a forever-young Marie Laveau. Photo by Bloody Mary © BMT, Inc.

Voodoo Yet Rules Faithful Disciples of Dead Sorceress Marie Laveau. Queen of the Voodoos in the 19th century New Orleans rites, died many years ago, but her ghost still lingers in the city and inspires a number of her faithful followers to make midnight pilgrimages to her tomb . . . Her grey ghost haunts the city which she imperiously ruled the Voodoo Rites . . .

—*Times-Picayune*, New Orleans, March 7, 1937

The Legacy

Now, to New Orleans's number-one called upon spirit, who flows through most all racial and religious barriers and also has the most visited tomb in the country: I present the internationally renowned Marie Laveau, the Voodoo queen. Her tomb, her life, and her afterlife haunt New Orleans throughout the ages in whispers and hushed tones in times of trouble and through troubadours by broad daylight telling her tales.

For eighty years on this earth, Marie Laveau's spirit raged on in the insurmountable odds of the real world of nineteenth-century New Orleans. And fifty-six years after her death, she was still consulted and making headlines. Now, 135 years after her death, she has more faithful disciples than ever. Her spirit is venerated and will continue to permeate New Orleans, as will the controversies about her life.

Nevertheless, 214 or so years ago, a star was born. Some say legends are born; others say they are made, but in many ways they are forged—tempered, heated, cooled, and transformed. This process continues in afterlife, for in spirit she is as strong as the iron her forebears forged in their ancient cauldron of life. And as in the sacred smithing of the ancient Africans, rituals surrounded the necessary process and offerings and sacrifices made along the way.

In the special case of Marie's legendary growth both before and after her physical death, she has reached beyond the limits of just New Orleans. There are many exalted ancestor Voodoo spirits in villages and tribes whose spirits are elevated as leaders and protectors of the bloodline served by their specific family Voodoo tradition who are unknown out of their particular region, but Marie Laveau has surpassed this "locals only" realm. She is known the world over and is called on as the popess of Voodoo.

She is an active spirit, and her ghost permeates New Orleans in legend and lore, music and magic, vision and apparition. This fact, along with her historic personage, has left an indelible imprint upon New Orleans. Add in the sheer number of people who visit her tomb and evoke her spirit, willingly or not, and she, in my estimation, is the number-one spirit called upon in North America outside the confines of the church, her canonized saints, and her intermediaries.

But just who is Marie Laveau? We have many ways to understand her—through legend, history, and supernatural knowing. And is she a ghost? Yes, by some definitions; but accurately she is more, a true mystery—a Voodoo, a spirit, loa, ascended master, sinner, and saint. All this and more describe this free woman of color who was born in 1801 in New Orleans.

But there really is more than one Marie Laveau: There is the living spirit, there is the living legend, and, of course, there is also the living flesh and blood . . .

The Legend

Marie Laveau ruled New Orleans as Voodoo queen for over a hundred years. A quadroon beauty, born of plaçage—a liaison between her momma and a local rich white planter, Charles Laveau Trudeau. He was connected with both church and state and taught her how to work "the man." She rose to power in Voodoo's heyday 'round 1830, climbing her way to the top, stopping at nothing. She was a political leader, a women's rights activist, and an abolitionist, too.

No one dared get in her way. She was ruthless and scheming, the perfect portrayal of desire du jour—the sorceress femme fatale. She did everything from magically banishing her rivals to physically beating them down in the streets. She was a sexual dynamo and a devout Catholic, too. She single-handedly combined the Catholic faith with Voodoo, and her charisma was as strong as she was psychically adept. Kings and queens of other lands sought her counsel in life and still do in afterlife. She had two husbands, many lovers, and fifteen children to boot.

Her love spells were so wondrous that a rich client gifted her a cottage in gratitude. She led rituals there and in Congo Square. Those Voodoo orgies, especially on St. John's Eve, were legendary displays of debauchery. The courts, judges, and policemen were all under Marie's control. She could make them bark like dogs if she wanted to, get 'em hired in one snap and fired in two.

She had a baby skeleton clinging to her armoire and a pet snake named Zombi. She consorted with crocodiles and danced with a fish. She stopped public executions by evoking a storm. She was an angel of mercy and a mercy killer to the condemned, "depending on the case." She made a killer gumbo, according to taste. She was said to be a midwife by day and an abortionist by night.

Her regular job as a hairdresser—a ruse—was just one way to get all the info she desired (and the hair, too!). She was updated by a slithering contortion of spies winding in and out of rich homes who sold her their secrets to enchant all to believe that she could read your mind. She would put spells on people just so they would come to her to have them removed.

She did anything to turn a buck, enticed young girls to her lair to turn a trick, bringing them girls down in dat *maison blanche* at the lake, where as procuress she would set them to a life of ruin. Her daughters grew to look just like her, and they finally continued her reign, granting her the glamour of the illusion of eternal youth.

She died in a big storm on the lake on her big day of St. John's, when she called on the "debbil" in the form of a snake. She had a big funeral with the who's who in attendance. Then her body was stolen, and her remains were buried and reburied again and again in at least four different cemeteries, particularly in St. Louis Cemetery No. 1. Here she still answers requests, grants wishes, heals ya, makes ya rich, and makes ya cry. She was and is forever Voodoo queen, known as the Voodoo Popess. She put a curse on this whole town. If you were born here, you can never really leave! And if you visit here, you always need to come back!

The Spirit

Paranormal signs, sights, apparitions, and healings have been reported at Marie Laveau's tomb shrine since her death in 1881. Marie Laveau is the number-one most called-upon spirit in New Orleans, the number-one most visited tomb in the country, and she is buried in St. Louis Cemetery No. 1 in the tomb marked "Famille Vve. Paris/née Laveau. ("Vve." is the French abbreviation for "widow." Jacques Paris was Marie's first husband; Christophe Glapion was her second.)

Marie's spirit work is not limited to her tomb, for she is venerated as a folk saint, a local adopted patron saint, ascended master, and a Voodoo spirit who is called on the world over . . . and she answers.

The spirit of Marie personally assists me and helps clients seeking cancer healing, surgical success, job acquisition, loan approval, protection for children, prevention of crime and injustice, and matters of the heart. She is credited for curing diseases. Even *The New York Times's* Stephen Kinzer covered such a story: "Interest Surges in Voodoo, and Its Queen." Here, a forty-one-year-old New York woman known as "Jackie" had been diagnosed with fatal meningitis but traveled to New Orleans "and made an offering at the tomb of Marie Laveau." After her visit, she reported a full recovery.

One of my clients, Robert Icenhour, reports that Marie has saved his life on three different occasions: a near suicide, a terrible car accident, and an operation gone seriously wrong. Her spirit interceded each time in deeds and apparition, with me also there at her side.

Marie Laveau's many supernatural feats are too long and too intricate to list here. To even scrape the surface of that iceberg, we would need to devote an entire book to her history, mystery, and magic.

Marie's spirit efficacy is multifaceted and undeniable to the hundreds of thousands who seek out her spirit work, in this country and around the world. She provides hope for many, with a renewed belief in miracles on top, and is a spiritual force to be reckoned with.

When Marie manifests, she communicates mainly with visuals and apports, delivering remedies directly to you. She stands beside those in need who call to her for assistance and intercedes to help her chosen ones even when not directly called. Her spirit has been seen at this tomb, at countless private altars, in her cottage property on St. Ann Street, at the bayou, and as an eyewitness-reported ghost at a Hoodoo drugstore on Rampart Street in the early twentieth century. It was reported by her contemporaries that she manifested as a Newfoundland dog, but other times she seems to prefer wearing the skin of a black cat. Both these creatures stalked her tomb in St. Louis Cemetery No. 1, and the dog allegedly burst into her funeral service at St. Louis Cathedral.

In modern day, Marie dresses quite differently. Long ago, she came to me dancing in an uncanny supernatural spotlight in order to direct "the lineage" my way. When I, and others, see Marie, she is very regal and has a beautiful glow, which appears saintly in aura. She is of few words, and she communicates through the power of gestures, signs, visions, and action.

She manifested over my client Clint's house in 2011 as a blue angel. We were building Marie's altar inside, and an out-and-out skeptic family member walking outside the house witnessed her hovering for more than fifteen minutes. Paranormal bells were heard inside and outside of the property starting then and continuing for several days. Marie has many ways of revealing herself.

The Life

This hard-working, very real, nineteenth-century native-born New Orleanian was a mother, wife, healer, devout Catholic, and spiritually connected free woman of color of moderate means. She, who was psychically gifted and very connected to the spirits of the land and the water, was also well versed in the psychology of all the peoples of her day. Marie was sought after for her incredible healing techniques of both body and soul. Laveau did her candle work in hybrid novena and folk magic style and prayed diligently with her Catholicism, shamanism, and Voodoo all in a row. She was a *traiteur*, or Creole folk healer; a medium, spirit controller, and true Voodoo Queen. She was also our Florence Nightingale who fought the fevers side by side with the Catholic Church.

1930s Louisiana Writers' Project (LWP) informant James St. Ann insists that "Marie Laveau was one of the mightiest queens in Louisiana . . . she could really do anything from curing your body and your mind."

She was sought after by many in life and afterlife—all races, all sexes, and all socioeconomic levels still flock to her. There have always been the more gifted seers and healers who worked closely with the spirits who became leaders, like Marie Laveau. Many people depended on Marie—all types came to her for this or that. But importantly, the spirits liked Marie, and she did have power. True power, not temporal power—just look at her now. That's real power, to still be "grown and known" so long after death.

Nathan Hobley, LWP informant, Hoodoo worker, and associate of Laveau, agrees:

But her power! It was supernatural!

She really did dance with a snake; she also danced with a fish, but she danced with the dead, too. Marie listened to the spirit of place, La Grande Zombi, and the Catholic saints, and she prayed directly to God. She also bound the devil back to keep evil spirits away. She listened to the swamp secrets from behind her grandma's cottage to the backbeat of Voodoo drums echoing from that nearby holy ground of Congo Square.

A writer for the LWP added these details about Marie's Voodoo rites of the time:

One of the voodoo songs states that the Queen, Marie Laveau, knew all kinds of gri-gri or charms, that she had gone to school with the crocodiles and the alligators, that she had a speaking acquaintance with The Grande Zombi, and that when the sun went down every evening in a little corner of the wild woods he would come out of the bayou to teach Marie Laveau all voodou mysteries . . . *"l'appe vini, li Grand Zombi! L'appe vini pur fa gri-gris!"*

Oral history says she showed the gift at a very young age. She was "a natural" and supernatural. Marie listened directly to all the chattering skeletons in the closets of the people in town and the voices from the graveyards, too. Her occult knowledge of African Voodoo was passed down to her from her elders and was mixed in with direct knowledge from the spirits, coworkers, Native American medicine people, and practical experience at hand.

LWP's Nathan Hobley describes her practices this way: "She used charms, herbs, incense, snakes, skeletons and invoked spirits." But what was her secret? She listened, she sacrificed, and she honored the spirits and the people. It boils down to this plain and simple thing—she was really good at what she did and became a star. She was known to be a very private, quiet person. You would have to really get to know her to earn her trust.

When misunderstood gifted powers exist within the chosen few, like Marie, weaker ones without such gifts seek to destroy and malign what they cannot understand. But those same people went to her when they were in trouble, and she still opened the way. Some loved Marie. Some feared Marie. Everyone respected Marie.

Jim Slater of the LWP adds the following:

De French and Spanish Doctors' ob dat time usta do hoodoo too. Some ob dem was wit Marie Laveau. I'm here ter tell you—dey had plenty dat follow her, but none of dem was as good as she was. Marie Laveau was er queen dat even da white folks was scared. An all dose dat followed her were jes two-headed folk. Dey sold der souls to de debbil and dey wouldn't stop at nothin'.

She inspired the Spiritualists and the Catholics. She was a good woman.

LWP informant Marie Dede added this about Marie:

Marie Laveau would not pray unless she prayed for hours. That was a praying woman. Saint Peter and Saint Anthony were her favorite saints. She did not do all that dirty work people say she did, no. You need a job, she get ya one. Hungry—she'd feed ya.

Other LWP informants corroborated the story:

Marie Laveau possessed the quality of self-sacrifice. She would give her last piece of money to a poor person. To every poor person that would come to her, a plate of food would be given and a place of rest would be provided.

Marie Laveau's youngest and only surviving child of her nine known children was Marie Philomene Glapion (Legendre). Some believe this Marie followed in her mother's footsteps as queen, but others believe it was a sister. I do not engage debate here and call upon the trinity of Maries instead. It was, however, this Marie who inherited the family tomb and interred her mamma with the name Dame Christophe Glapion. This little white lie went a long way. The word "Dame" would honor M. Philomene's natural father and further legitimize the Vve. Paris/Christophe Glapion liaison.

Christophe Glapion was Caucasian, and the couple was not married in the church's eyes. Their daughter, Marie Philomene, was concerned about her own children and future generations in the ever-changing, racially unjust world that she saw ahead, so she set the stage in 1881 with a bit of race subterfuge and some Voodoo denial on top. She was trying to clean up the family name in more ways than one. The multiple name usage also inadvertently became a source of confusion on where the real Marie Laveau is buried.

Marie is certainly not alone within, for she even provided a place of eternal rest for many deceased non–family members who are buried alongside her in her family tomb properties in St. Louis Cemetery No. 1. Marie Philomene followed this benevolent burial tradition as well. Archivist Carolyn Morrow Long has discovered 111 total burials in the three Laveau properties of St. Louis Cemetery No. 1: twenty-five family members and eighty-six non–family members. All races and all sexes, and over forty-five were babies. Eighty-six people are in the Vve. Paris shrine. (The other two tombs are not any of the fakelore ones pointed out to tourists in that cemetery.)

Marie and her daughter were philanthropists and quiet about it; they worked behind the scenes, like most mystic warriors do. The tomb shrine still provides food and money to the poor; it is a custom to recycle the offerings left there back to the community.

New Orleans is a wonderful but exceedingly jealous town. Marie lived through the most tumultuous times of plague, war, occupation, Reconstruction, and at the pinnacle of racial and social injustice. Marie didn't have it easy, but whether you are a queen, a priestess, or a latter-day saint, you reign to serve, not to have it easy. When you dedicate your life as priestess, you are a servant to the people and to the land. With this role comes great responsibility, which does not end at death.

Laveau's followers continued to call upon her spirit in ritual, at her special wishing spot on the bayou, and at power sites that she and her workers worshiped. Today, they continue to make

Marie showered with offerings.
Photo by Bloody Mary © BMT, Inc.

votive and ex-votive offerings and pilgrimages to her tomb to pray through her spirit. I continue in the traditional water baptisms, Marie Laveau Voodoo style, on June 23, St. John's Eve rituals at the lake, and she assists me as spirit guide throughout the entire year.

One's spirit grows in the afterlife. Catholics believe miracles performed after death count toward the worthiness of sainthood, coupled with the servitude and mystic qualities during their life. Envy and controversy around Marie's life, coupled with a lot of libel, muddied the modern Catholic Church's viewpoint of Marie to consider her for actual sainthood, for there seemed to be too many actual skeletons in her closet. She did work with bones, relics, and jujus, but in her day, Marie was readily accepted by the church and her priests. They did not read about Marie in later sensationalized books; they knew her. She remains a saint to many without official canonization and is a folk saint for all.

Marie's life was one of service, as is her afterlife. An elevation ritual would have been executed by her peers at least one year and a day after her death to draw Marie upward in the Voodoo spirit realm and assist her ascension to spiritual mother or loa.

Queen Marie is respected and venerated by countless adherents and is a primary spirit in my House. Marie is the ghost gatekeeper of New Orleans Voodoo, and the bridge that connects ancient African Voodoos to modern-day Voodoo. She is called on in private altars 'round the country and in several public shrines to her throughout the city, including my own.

Old man George Nelson, quoted in Catherine Dillon's 1940 unpublished LWP manuscript *Voodoo*, praises her:

> Marie Laveau was the wisest woman that ever lived. She was gifted with a power from on high that very few people are gifted with . . . she was in a way to me like another Solomon . . . I also picture her as John the Baptist who come here to teach right and righteousness. This woman . . . prayed not three times a day as Daniel did but prayed every hour of the day. . . . She was not selfish, but waited on de black as well as the white and the rich as well as the poor. Doing all the good she could, and never doing any harm to no body . . . she done for the people not of New Orleans but for the State of

Louisiana and the people of the United States, and I am told that the people came from foreign countries.

They still do.

Marie Catherine (Laveau) was born in New Orleans on September 10, 1794, and died June 15, 1881. Marie Laveau's obituary was even posted in *The New York Times* on June 23, 1881. She is buried where XXXs used to mark her spot.

The Lies

The controversies about Marie Laveau's life and death, and even where she is buried, are riddled with inconsistencies and imperfections, inflation and accusation, as well as hardship and heroism. Marie Laveau still teaches us how to persevere though all of life's unfairness, and she models strength though endurance. She is also the epitome of balance—yin and yang, the male and female. Marie is a survivor, and even through all of the hearsay and slander surrounding our exalted Voodoo Queen, she leaves us wading in a sense of wonder and awe.

In *Voodoo*, Catherine Dillon says the following:

> People used to go and ask favors on first Mondays, Wednesdays and Fridays ob da month—dey take red brick and knock on de tomb and make crosses. . . . X-shaped crosses . . . Present day Voodoos and other negroes insist that voodoo crosses are X's . . . many red brick crosses that indicate the burial place of a voodoo queen.

Archdiocese employee since 1919, sexton, and LWP informant Ayola Cruz clarifies more facts about Marie Laveau's tomb in St. Louis No. 1:

> Negroes and whites came almost daily to make offerings to Marie's spirit. They make crosses with red brick, charcoal and sharp rocks . . .

Cruz continues, verifiying that this exact Widow Paris tomb is also where "the real and only Marie Laveau is buried":

> The reason the tomb a so white is that they come a clean it— the son of the grandson's wife [widow Blair Legendre]. Many people come to a grave, bring a flowers and kneel down and pray. Some leave cooked foods, cake, breads, apples, even pineapples . . .

There were queens before Marie who were honored the same way, and since.

By the year 2005, rumor and negative publicity about the crossroads X marks on Marie Laveau's tomb were misconstrued as vandalism and made it to the press in *Times Picayune* articles from May 26–June 1. (One, by Lyne Jensen, was cleverly titled "Voodon't.") Many locals took up the X cross, and a rebuttal editorial was printed:

> [Voodon't is] a small group of citizens [attempting] to sanitize, whitewash and neuter the City of New Orleans . . . Marking Marie Laveau's tomb is an act of faith, not vandalism.

Continuing publicity brought more problems, and eventually the "neutering" led to banning both the Xs and the more important New Orleans tradition of votive and food offerings at the tomb.

A reverse fakelore circulated by a few citizens trying to deny any cultural or spiritual significance of the Xs added more mistruths that the custom started locally only in the late twentieth century. The lies were an attempt to curtail the abundance of X markings. These Voodon't's came armed with misquotes from unidentified and unresearched Voodoo practitioners and a few alleged owners of the Laveau tomb denouncing the custom. It became the Voodoos versus the Voodon'ts.

The Laveau/Legendre tomb is officially of untitled ownership and is designated as no-name status (abandoned), with no living direct descendants to claim. The last living direct descendent was unavailable for direct interview when I inquired at her nursing home for comment in 2005. Ethel Legendre Karl died Feb 18, 2005, at the age of ninety-two in Hancock County, Mississippi. According to her obituary, "She is survived by several cousins and good friends." She had no children. Ethel lived the last year of her life under the benevolence of her friends Michael and Micki of Bay St. Louis, who were very surprised to hear of Ethel's famous Laveau lineage when we spoke. Ethel did not confide this information to her good friends even in her last days. Ethel was seemingly unaware of her ownership rights to the Laveau/Legendre tomb and may have not have known she was related to the late, great Marie Laveau. Ethel Legendre was designated Caucasian, was Catholic, and was an honored member of the Order of the Eastern Star. She was Marie Laveau's great-great-granddaughter and Marie Philomene's great-granddaughter. Philomene had successfully whitewashed her family tree starting in 1881, and her direct lineage died out in 2005, taking that secret with Ethel to the grave.

The last recorded Laveau/Legendre tomb opening in 1917 was ordered by the last official titled owner, Blair Legendre, M. Philomene's son. There was a 1957 non-recorded owner burial, too. Blair's wife Rose Legendre and son Ceril were the last family member tomb caretakers. The existing Glapion Louisiana branch are not descendants of Christophe Glapion or Marie Lavaeu and have no inheritance rights or tomb restoration obligations. Any cleaning, whitewashing, and restoration for the past fifty years has been done from non-family sources. Marie Laveau was Blair Legendre's grandmother.

Of New Orleans–born grandmothers, 9.9 out of 10 agree that the Xs are tradition at Marie Laveau's grave. I personally first heard of this practice on the playground in first grade. Ethnologists agree that the African diaspora tradition of Xs as crossroads marks is significant and widespread throughout the world. In North America, Xs are found mainly in New Orleans, and the meaning of the cross marks has been misconstrued here only in the past thirteen years. Most locals grew up understanding the cross marks as the Voodoo crossroads cosmogram, which is validated in a 1993 study by Grey Gundaker in *Signs of Diaspora*:

> St. Louis Cemetery Number One . . . devotees have
> scratched cross marks to seal requests made to the spirits . . .
> In New Orleans, there seems to be a fairly general agreement
> about the significance of cross marks on tombs.

A decade after this study, a small group of preservationists in a backward attempt to keep the tomb clean started the rally to ban the Xs. The butterfly effect had begun. And a decade after that, the majority of imported tour guides and gullible locals—especially the newer post-Katrina transplants—swallowed the X ban wholeheartedly. Some guides even took self-appointed militant approaches in the graveyard, verbally assaulting and frightening elderly women away when they tried to pray at the tomb, as their forbearers had done. Others were condescending, childishly pointing and laughing at those paying homage to and seeking help from Marie. The Catholic Church never took such an approach. They loved Marie Laveau in life, wrote matter-of-factly about the X tradition in their own cemetery book, and in an awkward way they are protecting her still: The Laveau/Legendre tomb is appropriately numbered "3" in the archdiocese's map of notable tombs.

In their 1961 book, *The St. Louis Cemeteries of New Orleans*, Samuel Wilson and Leonard Huber confirm this tradition:

> Marie Laveau['s] remains, identified as Widow Paris, reputedly rest in a tomb much marked for good luck with "X's" of visitors.

These X-prohibition attempts backfired and the tomb got indelibly marked more than ever, culminating in a confused devotee sneaking into St. Louis Cemetery No. 1 in late December 2013 and painting Marie's tomb a "Pepto-Bysmal" pink. An unnecessary media duel ensued in response to outside sources condemning the quality of the archdiocese's pressure-washing efforts. The situation seemed whitewashed in totality by Halloween 2014 with the unveiling of Marie's ten-thousand-dollar newly restored tomb.

Yet all the unwanted controversy and publicity coupled with a later, seemingly unrelated, break-in forced the hand of the archdiocese to make a more dramatic countermove, and alas, the bishop took the queen.

The closure of the cemetery to the public flooded many New Orleanians and devotees with sorrow. Marie's sturdy three-vault Greek revival family tomb existed in far better shape than most of the abandoned tombs in the old St. Louis Cemetery whose ground is littered with broken brick and mortar from the neglect of time and lack of maintenance. Now it stands, restored, stark naked: with no décor, no offerings, no Xs, and no flavor!

I agree with many cemetery owners interviewed for the New Orleans website *NOLAdeadspace.com* on the subjects of vandalism and desecration that downplaying publicity of such problems and upgrading education of local customs are potential solutions: "They shun publicity on the problem, as they believe that press coverage just encourages more juvenile destructive behaviour."

Preserving traditions through truthful education, not denial, is a vital part of maintaining one's culture and instilling pride. It is even sadder to destroy a tradition's sacred roots simply to appease someone's agenda.

The sign of the cross can be made on your body, in the air, or on the earthen ground, and this will still solicit Marie's help. I firmly believe if more people had chosen to teach proper implementation of these sacred customs with due respect to the tomb, none of this would have happened. Prohibition rarely works. Natural brick chalk Xs washed away easily in the rain for about 150 years, but the waxy red lipstick of modern tourists does not.

The Laveau ceremony: Knock three times, spin three too, counterclockwise will do. Face the tomb and make the sign of the cross. Orient your offerings to all four corners and pray, petition, listen for the answer to come your way. Leave your gifts, give thanks, then close the way. Knock three more times, scrape your foot for three or clap three for Papa Labas to close the way.

Let me defer to native-born elder Voodoo priestess and author Luisah Teish's response to me in her soulful words:

> The tomb of Mam'zelle Marie LaVeau is one of the most sacred places in New Orleans. Since childhood I'd heard elders say that Mam'zelle's spirit was active in heaven looking down on those of us who had the gift, the eyes to see, the ears to hear, and most of all the courage to face the responsibility of fulfilling a promise to spirit.
>
> This was not talked about the way one discussed holiday dinners or recent births. No. No. It was whispered during troubled times: when a child had been molested, when precious property had been stolen, when sleepless nights sapped energy . . . when the Klan was on the rise. At these times, the eavesdropping child could overhear the elders (mostly women) formulate remedies with speckled hens, brick dust and visits to the tomb of Mam'zelle Marie LaVeau.
>
> I mark my X, the sign of the crossroads, the universal four directions, the balance of the human body in wide-legged stance with arms extended. I mark with red brick, the clay and water of the Mississippi, used to build homes, cleanse wood and seam stone. I shower the tomb with coins

and flowers and sing songs to the ancestors. Divination provides an affirmative answer. And I am grateful.

This practice of invoking Mam'zelle comes to me from the late 1800's. It is not a new invention. Whosoever imagines that they can advertise otherwise is a clown and a deceiver. Many attempts have been made for generations to wipe out the ways of common folks. But it only serves to compress the power, which always rises again generation after generation.

I stand firm and clear on the evidence of my culture and my personal experience regarding the efficacy of the spirit of Mam'zelle Marie LaVeau and the practice of visiting, feeding and the age old tradition of the X's as a sacred important part of New Orleans, as an old and noble symbol and I testify her tomb shrine as a holy site to visit for guidance and assistance and as a right for all in need.

Marie Laveau: Saint Marie of the Swamp; patron saint of New Orleanians, women's mysteries, cultural preservation, and New Orleans Voodoo.

The Spirits' Who's Who

- **Ascended Master/Saint**—Marie Laveau falls into this category as an ascended master/saint. She is our Voodoo, mysterie, spirit, or loa, and a New Orleans patron saint who watches over us, healing and acting as intermediary. She is undeniably a folk saint who is venerated and petitioned for help by the masses. Miracles are made at her side. She is also a teacher.

- **Living Shrine**—Places of power that are alive with spirit. Marie's tomb is a living shrine, an altar in itself and a New Orleans sanctum sanctorum, a holy of holies. The sacred bones within act like holy relics, empowering the area and helping those who pilgrimage near there to petition for help through her intercessory spirit.

- **Phantom of the Living**—A piece of a living person's spirit can sometimes be seen just like a ghost when it is a projection from a living human. This can be intentional, as sent through astral travel or an out-of-body experience, or accidental, through some form of trauma-induced split. They can be seen like a duplicate or phantom of the living person. I have been seen this way or heard by some of my clients while I was remotely cleansing their house.

✦

Afterlife Lessons

Some spirits are funny, wily, even seductive; or, like Marie, profoundly wise and helpful.

Spirits can be ascended masters in their field; some are spirit guides, escorts, or just regular residents; and only a few are truly stuck. Remember, no one ever said heaven is a jail, and many of our friends and family become our spirit guides.

Marie Laveau and Bloody Mary at her mid-city Spirit Realm Shrine to the Voodoo Queen featuring a full-sized terracotta Marie statue displayed in a swamp environ. Photo by Matthew Pouliot © BMT, Inc.

Marie's tomb is a microcosm of modern times, reflecting the bigger picture of religion at large where many people go through the motions of rituals without knowing the meaning behind them. The whys are important. Seek the source.

✦

Warnings

Approach ancestors with respect.

Speak true of the dead.

Be careful how you word invitations to the spirit world—they may take you literally.

Sometimes it's not *what* you ask, but *how* you ask.

Be ready to have your questions and prayers answered.

Do not ask and then ignore the grace bestowed.

Lies eventually find their source.

Lies about Marie's work began during her lifetime, legends were exaggerated further in early twentieth-century books, and stories continue today in mammoth proportions. Modern websites, unethically edited documentaries, many tour guides, and some TV dramas are fictionalizing the Laveau legend, and her folklore is rapidly becoming ridiculous "Fakelore". These lies can cross over to reach the spirit of Marie Laveau.

There are many ways to handle situations to make it a win-win, truthfully, without aggression, desecration, or lies. A chaos theory suggests that repercussions can emanate from a single occurrence and spread exponentially. This butterfly effect affects the physical and the spiritual planes. Beware of what you say about the dead; they are listening and it matters.

My hometown is an important port town on both sides of the veil—port and portal. The living and the dead just keep rolling in and out. (No wonder New Orleans is so haunted!) Large influxes of newcomers import and export themselves from this place, taking a little and giving a little in the process as time marches on.

There is a renaissance of the flesh and the spirit in post-Katrina New Orleans. But with this comes danger—a danger of losing some of our customs and memories, as massive sets of newcomers move in who do not have generations of family members who molded these things, live and in-person as we, the Creoles, did. They are attracted by the primal and spirit-filled creative energies here, and yet they want to rewrite us. Their footsteps are deep, and the results lie in a new New Orleans book waiting to be written. This was the preface, for we are at that crossroads right now.

True proof of the afterlife is found only in your personal experience. Just remember to help the living and the dead—a kind word, a prayer, or even a joke to break the ice. Remember the spirits' humanness, and so will they. Also, remember your responsibilities when those doors open, for it could be a dark entry and you may need to be the one who knows how to close them.

Conclusion

THANK YOU FOR SHARING this journey with me as I introduced you to my many multidimensional neighbors. All of them have something to teach us, even if they are dark. Yet, I still contend that there is more of the wondrous surrounding us than the other. But either way, "Fear Not" is my motto.

Our out-of-flesh citizens come forward for myriad reasons. Some can be earning their wings, while others are intentional stay-behinds who return to remedy a specific situation. Specialty cases create ascended masters or saint-type spirits like Marie Laveau, angel moms like my mom, and a couple of Cupids and a baby cherub were highlighted, too. Others may simply want to watch over as guardians and choose to protect people or spirit-guard places. Some just continue their life's work or are visitors. We are all assigned jobs on the other side. The roles of *le morte* are plentiful. These could be your own ancestors, assigned guardians, docents or caretakers of a sacred space, and even elementals or otherworldly beings that you run into.

Of course, some are *suckeurs*, those many-named, draining, dark ones—maybe that's all they knew in life, and so become magnetic vampires after; maybe they are amoral and better classified as survival-primordial. Perhaps these spirits were never born in the flesh at all—bottom-feeder types. All kinds just come and go, back and forth—some just because they can. I believe only a few are truly stuck and only a few are truly dark. My aim for you is to model strength in the face of darkness and help you conquer fears—or act in spite of them.

Studies of the afterlife, in-between life, and multidimensional existence are plentiful. Many scholars before me have devoted much time assimilating supernatural phenomena within this mortal realm of ours. I have studied many prior doctrines, yet I have my own philosophy derived directly from spirit-source teachings and experience. I also have personally witnessed and facilitated countless soul-healing processes and achieved success time and time again and learned from a few failures. I must also reiterate that time itself, to us and to them, is not the same; neither are space and distance; as we know it, they know it differently. Consider also that the sides we speak of are not such separate places, but more of a fluid multidimensional matrix.

Just open up and learn from each other, if you can, and be patient. Patience is a virtue and we should not rush into these things foolhardily. Develop your own relationship with the many spirit realms around us, over time. Connection is not always easy, and rarely is it quick. Don't expect immediate answers and connection with the spirit world and your place in it. Make the time to develop your own particular gifts. Some people may never be able to see a ghost, but they might hear, feel, or sense one. It is about both the sender and the receiver's capabilities. The worlds are like a kaleidoscope with ever-changing facets shown to us in pieces like a puzzle that we need to learn to put together to get the big picture. Every turn we take reveals a different view.

Regardless if connection is your goal or not, it is good advice to fear not, be strong, and be aware. We should strive in this lifetime to be everything we came here to be while we are alive, as best as we can. We should teach, learn, love, and care for our family and our world as much as we can. Some of us realize our potential while in the flesh; others do not. Some could be a little lost on the other side and may need our assistance as they still grow and ascend in their in-between lives; we simply need to consider that and assist. This time is called the inter-life more specifically than the afterlife because most of us will be born again. Whatever you call it, there is this time in between—the crossroads time—where there just may be a second chance.

Spirits have the right to live amongst us, and most of them were here first anyway. We should learn to live and help each other just like a family. Sure, we may have different points of view occasionally, and personal boundaries may need to be negotiated; but if we cooperate, we can create harmony and understanding. It could also add a little bit of awe and purpose to this life at the same time.

I salute our spirit brothers and sisters, break bread with them, and try to consider their needs, fears, and limitations, as well as appreciate their wisdom. I also believe it should be a two-way street. I even turn the other cheek; but if real danger threatens me, my family, or my city, I am a relentless warrior with a mighty sword, and I have an army who stands with me. I don't break out the big guns unless I have to (and I have had to).

Do not wage war with things just because they are different from you, but defend yourself when necessary. Most of the time the shield is mightier than the sword, but it is wise to keep your wits sharpened and your weapons readied.

Leap into the void full of faith, carrying your fears and apprehensions as insignificantly as dirt on the soles of your shoes. But clean out your own closets first, know thyself, respect our spirit allies, and remember to ground so you can live a full life. If, along the way, you lend a hand to help a brother or sister, in the flesh or in between, it will lighten the load of the many worlds' journeys and balance the scales.

I advise most people not to quit their day jobs, because your work helps you ground. Try to keep strong in your spirituality, and redeem your mistakes while in the flesh. Be strong in body and mind, for you will be tested and tempted along your path. This calling is not a game or a hobby. You may take a wrong turn or need to be redirected as you grow, for there is a need for you to advance spiritually. Challenges and tests will come; sometimes you need to fight and sometimes you need to surrender, be torn apart, and built anew.

Do not look at this as a curse; this is an opportunity to grow. You also need to face your own demons in the process. In the long run, the spirits are teaching you. It is a form of direct initiation—they can help break you down, rebuild, and transform. Expect this to occur. You might get a forced incubation time-out if you do not heed the gentle signs for your soul to fight for the right of advancement. Rites of passage, shamanic crises, dark nights of the soul, and ritual initiations are all opportunities to advance your soul in its endeavors to be reborn. Life has built in tests, trials, and tribulations to guide you. Endurance makes you stronger.

There is a polyrhythm out there that may require the breaking of old patterns and a resting time. During the tuning part, things may sound a bit sour as they move toward that perfect chord. It's all in how you work with the strings that provides the key to harmony.

Either way, this is your incarnation and you are the master of your destiny. Make the right choices and fear not, and simply apply caution, for there is a dark side; just offer it none of your power and put it in check.

In New Orleans, and in all my travels, I touch sacred sites, explore haunted sites, and share spirit knowledge along the way. My whole life is a supernatural mission. My whole life is this dance. I cannot separate this from who I am. There really is no separation of the sacred and the mundane.

Bibliography

Books

Asbury, Herbert. *The French Quarter: An Informal History of the New Orleans Underworld.* New York: Alfred A. Knopf, 1936.

Basso, Etolia S., ed. *The World from Jackson Square (A New Orleans Reader).* New York: Farrar, Straus & Company, 1948.

Bookhardt, D. Eric, and Jon Newlin. *Wonders of New Orleans.* New Orleans: Temperance Hall, 1992.

Braude, Anna. *Radical Spirits: Spiritualism and Women's Rights in Nineteenth-Century America.* Bloomington, IN: Indiana University Press, 2001.

Cable, George W. *Strange True Stories of Louisiana.* Gretna, LA: Pelican Publishing, 1994. Reissue.

Cable, Mary. *Lost New Orleans.* Boston: Houghton Mifflin, 1980.

Christian, Marcus. *Negro Ironworkers of Louisiana, 1718–1900.* Gretna, LA: Pelican Publishing, 1972

Davis, William C. *The Pirates Laffite: The Treacherous World of the Corsairs of the Gulf.* Orlando, FL: Harcourt, 2006.

deLavigne, Jeanne. *Ghost Stories of Old New Orleans.* New York: Rinehart and Co., Inc., J. J. Little and Ives, 1946.

Ebeyer, Pierre Paul. *Paramours of the Creoles of Old New Orleans.* New Orleans: Windmill Publishing, 1944.

Gayarré, Charles. *History of Louisiana.* New York: William J. Widdleton, 1867.

Gundaker, Grey. *Signs of Diaspora/Diaspora of Signs: Literacies, Creolization, and Vernacular Practice in African America.* Oxford, England: Oxford University Press, 1998.

Huber, Leonard V., Peggy McDowell, and Mary Louise Christovich. *New Orleans Architecture, Volume III: The Cemeteries.* Gretna, LA: Pelican Publishing, 1997.

Holzer, Hans. *Ghosts: True Encounters with the World Beyond.* New York: Aspera Ad Astra, Inc., 1997.

Klein, Victor C. *New Orleans Ghosts.* Chapel Hill, NC: Lycanthrope Press, 1993.

Laffite, Jean. *The Memoirs of Jean Laffite.* Translated by Gene Marshall. Brandon, MS: Dogwood Press, 1994.

Long, Carolyn Morrow. *A New Orleans Voudou Priestess: The Legend and Reality of Marie Laveau.* Gainesville: University Press of Florida, 2007.

———. *Madame Lalaurie: Mistress of the Haunted House.* Gainesville: University Press of Florida, 2012.

Martineau, Harriet. *Retrospect of Western Travel.* London: Saunders and Otley, 1838.

Penczak, Christopher. *Ascension Magick: Ritual, Myth & Healing for the New Aeon.* Woodbury, MN: Llewellyn, 2007.

Pritchard, Walter, ed. *The Louisiana Historical Quarterly* 29, no. 3 (July 1936).

Reneaux, J. J. *Haunted Bayou and Other Cajun Ghost Stories.* Little Rock, AR: August House, 1994.

Rose, Al. *Storyville, New Orleans.* Tuscaloosa, AL: University of Alabama Press, 1974.

Saxon, Lyle, Edward Dreyer, and Robert Tallant. *Gumbo Ya-Ya: A Collection of Louisiana Folk Tales.* Gretna, New York: Crown Publishing, 1945.

Stelwagon, Henry Weightman. *A Treatise on Diseases of the Skin for the Use of Advanced Students and Practitioners,* 4th edition. Philadelphia and London: W.B. Saunders and Co., 1905.

Teish, Luisah. *Jambalaya: The Natural Woman's Book of Personal Charms and Practical Rituals.* New York: HarperCollins, 1988.

Wilson, Samuel, and Leonard Huber. *The St. Louis Cemeteries of New Orleans.* New Orleans: St. Louis Cathedral, 1963.

Wlodarski, Robert, and Anne Wlodarski. *Louisiana Hauntspitality.* Alton, IL: Whitechapel Productions, 2004.

Newspapers

The New York Times
The Sun Herald (Biloxi, MS)
The Sea Coast Echo (Bay St. Louis, MS)

New Orleans papers:

Louisiana Gazette (1817–1826)

Moniteur de la Louisiane (1794–1815)

The Courier = Le Courrier (1824–18??)

The Crusader (1889–189?)

The Daily Picayune (1837–1914)

The Louisiana Gazette and New-Orleans Advertiser (1812–1815)

The New Orleans Bee

The States-Item

The Times-Democrat (1881–1914)

The Times-Picayune

Special Collections and Archives

Archdiocese Archives. Special thanks to Phillip Nolan.

Federal Writers' Project

Louisiana Writers' Project (LWP). Catherine Dillon, *Voodoo*, unpublished LWP manuscript.

Loyola University Library Special Collections

Missouri History Museum, DeLauss-St. Vrain Letter Collection, 1842

New Orleans Archives. Special thanks to Juliet.

NOLA Public Library Main Branch, Loyola Ave. Louisiana Special Collections

Northwestern State University of Louisiana; Watson Memorial Library, Cammie G. Research Center

Tulane University, Howard Tilton Library, LaRC NOLA

University of New Orleans Library, Earl K. Long Special Collections: Louisiana Collection

Williams Research Center NOLA, New Orleans Collection

Websites

Bloody Mary, "New Orleans History," Bloody Mary's Tours, www.bloodymarystours.com/hist-cemeteries.html.

Chris Chatfield, "Miasma: The Blue Mist Mystery," The Gallery of Natural Phenomena, http://www.phenomena.org.uk/features/features/miasma.html.

Patricia Leigh Brown, "New Orleans Grave Theft: Nothing's Sacred," *The New York Times*, February 16, 1999, http://www.nytimes.com/1999/02/16/us/new-orleans-grave-theft-nothing-s-sacred.html.

Shahid Raza Shalid et al., "Ghost Spell or Hematohidrosis," *Journal of the College of Physicians and Surgeons—Pakistan* 23, no. 4 (April 2013), 293–, http://www.researchgate.net/publication/236103571_Ghost_spell_or_hematohidrosis.

"The Dead Voudou Queen," *The New York Times*, June 23, 1881, http://query.nytimes.com/mem/archive-free/pdf?res=9E07E3DD103CEE3ABC4B51DFB066838A699FDE.

http://nolacatholiccemeteries.org/tourism/

www.nolodeadspace.com

About the Author

Bloody Mary is New Orleans's number-one celebrity historian of her hometown's supernatural past. As a born-and-raised NOLA gal, she shares both her unique women's historic perspective and an insider's knowledge drawn from family roots reaching back ten generations. She grew up immersed in the folklore of New Orleans, spent her adulthood researching the facts behind the lore, and connects firsthand with the spirits themselves as a gifted intuitive medium. She is also a revered folk historian, paranormal photographer, acclaimed storyteller, and internationally renowned documentarian appearing in hundreds of television shows about NOLA.

Bloody Mary opened America's first Ghost Photo Gallery in 1999 and has been teaching spirit communication connection techniques for over twenty years. She tours the country as an inspirational speaker promoting the Voodoo Paranormal technique and ancestral wisdom as an important and ne'er forgotten part of the worlds around us. She is an international advocate for spirit rights and is an industry leader in her field.

As Voodoo Queen, Mary heads her own New Orleans Voodoo family tradition temple and works side by side with her spirit guide, Marie Laveau. She presides over Voodoo rituals, weddings, ghost hunts, paranormal investigations, and, of course, her world-famous tours.

Mary lives in New Orleans with her husband Matthew and son Jagger along with their two dogs, one cat, several reptiles, and a house full of ghosts. The whole family works together in Bloody Mary's Tours and Spirit Realm, where they explore the spiritual worlds together as a team.

To Our Readers